COLLOQUIUM BIBLICUM LOVANIENSE
1-50

COLLOQUIUM BIBLICUM LOVANIENSE

Journées Bibliques de Louvain
Bijbelse Studiedagen te Leuven

1-50

1949-2001

Edited by F. Neirynck

LEUVEN
UNIVERSITY PRESS

UITGEVERIJ PEETERS
LEUVEN - PARIS - STERLING, VA

2001

STUDIORUM NOVI TESTAMENTI AUXILIA
XIX

ISBN 90 5867 150 X (Leuven University Press)
D/2001/1869/55
ISBN 90-429-1045-3 (Uitgeverij Peeters)
D. 2001/0602/67

Leuven University Press / Presses Universitaires de Louvain
Universitaire Pers Leuven
Blijde Inkomststraat 5, B-3000 Leuven-Louvain (Belgium)

© Uitgeverij Peeters, Bondgenotenlaan 153, B-3000 Leuven (Belgium)

CONTENTS

Colloquium Biblicum Lovaniense 1-50

Abbreviations 8
Chronological Table 1949-2001 9-10
Published Volumes 11-100
List of Contributors 101-108
BETL 109-116

Frontispiece: College Paus Adrianus VI. Lithograph J.B. Jobard (1830).

ABBREVIATIONS

CBL   Colloquium Biblicum Lovaniense

ALBO   Analecta Lovaniensia Biblica et Orientalia
BETL   Bibliotheca Ephemeridum Theologicarum Lovaniensium
ETL   Ephemerides Theologicae Lovanienses
OBL   Orientalia et Biblica Lovaniensia
RechB Recherches Bibliques
SNTA Studiorum Novi Testamenti Auxilia

Colloquium Biblicum Lovaniense
1949-2001

PRESIDENT

1.	1949	L. Cerfaux	Le sens des Écritures	ALBO II/16
2.	1950	J. Coppens	La théologie biblique	
3.	1951	J. Levie	L'enseignement de l'exégèse	
4.	1952	B. Rigaux	L'attente du Messie	RechB 1
5.	1953	P. Van Imschoot	La piété biblique	
6.	1954	G. Ryckmans	L'Ancien Testament et l'Orient	OBL 1
7.	1955	J. Heuschen	La formation des évangiles	RechB 2
8.	1956	F.-M. Braun	L'évangile de Jean	RechB 3
9.	1957	J. van der Ploeg	La secte de Qumrân	RechB 4
10.	1958	J. Coppens	Congressus Internationalis Catholicus	BETL 12-13
11.	1959	A. Descamps	Littérature et théologie pauliniennes	RechB 5
12.	1960	R. De Langhe	Le Psautier	OBL 4
13.	1961	E. Massaux	La venue du Messie	RechB 6
14.	1962	J. Giblet	Aux origines de l'Église	RechB 7
15.	1963	C. Hauret	L'Ancien Testament	RechB 8
	1964	(SNTS Meeting)		
16.	1965	I. de la Potterie	De Jésus aux évangiles	BETL 25
17.	1966	G. Thils - R.E. Brown	Exégèse et théologie	BETL 26
18.	1967	H. Cazelles	De Mari à Qumrân	BETL 24
19.	1968	F. Neirynck	L'évangile de Luc	BETL 32
20.	1969	W.C. van Unnik	Entre Tenach et Mischna	RechB 9
21.	1970	M. Didier	L'évangile selon Matthieu	BETL 29
22.	1971	M. Sabbe	L'évangile selon Marc	BETL 34
23.	1972	C. Brekelmans	Ancien Testament	BETL 33
24.	1973	J. Dupont	Jésus aux origines de la christologie	BETL 40
25.	1974	J. Coppens	La notion biblique de Dieu	BETL 41
26.	1975	M. de Jonge	L'évangile de Jean	BETL 44
27.	1976	M. Delcor	Qumrân	BETL 46
28.	1977	J. Kremer	Les Actes des Apôtres	BETL 48
29.	1978	M. Gilbert	La Sagesse dans l'Ancien Testament	BETL 51
30.	1979	J. Lambrecht	L'Apocalypse johannique	BETL 53
31.	1980	P.-M. Bogaert	Le livre de Jérémie	BETL 54
32.	1981	J. Delobel	Logia. Les paroles de Jésus	BETL 59
	1982	(SNTS Meeting)		
33.	1983	N. Lohfink	Das Deuteronomium	BETL 68
34.	1984	A. Vanhoye	L'Apôtre Paul	BETL 73
35.	1985	J. Lust	Ezekiel and his Book	BETL 74
36.	1986	J.-M. Sevrin	The NT in Early Christianity	BETL 86
37.	1987	J. Vermeylen	The Book of Isaiah	BETL 81
38.	1988	R.F. Collins	The Thessalonian Correspondence	BETL 87
	1989	(IOSOT Congress)		

39. 1990	A. Denaux	John and the Synoptics	BETL 101
40. 1991	A.S. van der Woude	The Book of Daniel	BETL 106
41. 1992	C. Focant	The Synoptic Gospels	BETL 110
42. 1993	W.A.M. Beuken	The Book of Job	BETL 114
43. 1994	R. Bieringer	The Corinthian Correspondence	BETL 125
44. 1995	M. Vervenne	The Book of Exodus	BETL 126
45. 1996	C.M. Tuckett	The Scriptures in the Gospels	BETL 131
46. 1997	A. Schoors	Qohelet	BETL 136
47. 1998	J. Verheyden	Luke-Acts	BETL 142
48. 1999	A. Wénin	The Book of Genesis	BETL 155
49. 2000	A. Lindemann	The Sayings Source Q	BETL 158
50. 2001	J.-M. Auwers H.J. de Jonge	The Biblical Canons	BETL

COLLOQUIUM BIBLICUM LOVANIENSE

1 1949 ix. 7-8

Sensus plenarius Scripturae Sacrae.
Président: L. CERFAUX

J. COPPENS (éd.), *Problèmes et méthode d'exégèse théologique.*
(ALBO, II/16), Leuven-Brugge, 1950, 91 p.

J. COPPENS (Leuven), Avant-propos	7-9
J. COPPENS, Le problème d'un sens biblique plénier	11-19
J. GRIBOMONT (Clervaux), Sens plénier, sens typique et sens littéral[1]	21-31
L. CERFAUX (Louvain), Simples réflexions à propos de l'exégèse apostolique[2]	33-34
J. COPPENS, Le protévangile. Un nouvel essai d'exégèse[3]	45-77
J. COPPENS, Bibliographie	79-90

1. *ETL* 25 (1949) 577-587.
2. *ETL* 25 (1949) 565-576; *Recueil Lucien Cerfaux*, II (BETL, 7), Gembloux, 1954, 189-203.
3. *ETL* 26 (1950) 5-36.

Addendum: P. SAMAIN, *Note sur le sens spirituel des Écritures*, in *Revue diocésaine de Tournai* 3 (1948) 429-433.

ix. 11-12
2 1950

La théologie biblique.
Cf. *ETL* 26 (1950) 552-554.

J. COPPENS, B.L. van Helmond, P. Van Imschoot, B. Alfrink, B. Rigaux, A. Charue

3 1951 ix. 3-5

L'enseignement de l'exégèse aux séminaires.
Cf. *ETL* 27 (1951) 693-696.

J. LEVIE, J. Coppens, J. Cambier, N. Schneider, G. Lambert, A. Lefèvre, A. Descamps, L. Cerfaux

4 1952 ix. 1-3

B. RIGAUX (éd.), *L'attente du Messie.*
(Recherches Bibliques, 1), Brugge, 1954, ²1958, 189 p.

A.-M. CHARUE (évêque de Namur), Avant-propos 9-11
B. RIGAUX (Bruxelles), Préface 13-14
B. RIGAUX, L'étude du messianisme. Problèmes et méthodes 15-30
J. COPPENS (Leuven), Les origines du messianisme. La synthèse historique de M. Sigmund Mowinckel 31-38
J. COPPENS, La prophétie d'Emmanuel 39-50
V. DE LEEUW (Udenhout), Le Serviteur de Jahvé. Figure royale ou prophétique? 51-56
A. DESCAMPS (Tournai), Le messianisme royal dans le Nouveau Testament 57-84
J. GIBLET (Malines), Prophétisme et attente d'un Messie-prophète dans le Judaïsme 85-130
L. CERFAUX (Louvain), Les miracles, signes messianiques de Jésus et œuvres de Dieu, selon l'évangile de S. Jean[1] . 131-138
J. COPPENS, La christologie de saint Paul 139-153
R. DE LANGHE (Leuven), Judaïsme ou hellénisme en rapport avec le Nouveau Testament 154-183
Conclusions 184-186
Bibliographie 187-188

1. *Recueil Lucien Cerfaux*, II (BETL, 7), Gembloux, 1954, 41-50.

Addendum: W. GROSSOUW, *Rudolf Bultmann en het vierde evangelie*, in *Studia Catholica* 28 (1953) 2-19; J. VAN DER PLOEG, *Profetie en vervulling*, ibid., 81-93.

5 1953 viii. 30 - ix. 1

La piété biblique.
Cf. *ETL* 29 (1953) 699.

P. VAN IMSCHOOT, H. Van den Bussche, J. De Fraine, W. Grossouw, A. Gelin, B. Van de Walle, G. Vermes, L. Cerfaux

6 1954

G. Ryckmans (éd.), *L'Ancien Testament et l'Orient.*
(Orientalia et Biblica Lovaniensia, 1), Leuven, 1957, 231 p.

G. Ryckmans (Leuven), Allocution d'ouverture de la VIᵉ
session 1-3
A.M. van Dijk (Leiden), La découverte de la culture littéraire
sumérienne et sa signification pour l'histoire de l'anti-
quité orientale 5-28
J.M.A. Janssen (Leiden), À travers les publications égypto-
logiques récentes concernant l'Ancien Testament . . . 29-63
R. De Langhe (Leuven), La Bible et la littérature ugaritique 65-78
G. Ryckmans, L'Arabie antique et la Bible 89-109
A. Guillaume (London), L'apport de la langue et des tradi-
tions arabes à l'interprétation de l'Ancien Testament . 111-121
G.R. Driver (Oxford), Glosses in the Hebrew Text of the
Old Testament 123-161
G. Dossin (Liège), Une *lectio difficilior* dans *Juges*, IX, 31 . 163-167
E.J. Kissane (Maynooth), «Butter and Honey Shall He Eat»
(*Is.*, 7:15) 169-173
H.H. Rowley (Manchester), Sanballat et le temple samari-
tain [1] 175-191
F.-M. Braun (Fribourg-en-Suisse), Le Mandéisme et la secte
essénienne de Qumrân 193-230

1. *Sanballat and the Samaritan Temple*, in *Men of God. Studies in Old Testament History and Prophecy*, London, 1963, 246-276.

Addendum: A. Descamps, *La carrière scientifique de Monseigneur Cerfaux*, in *ETL* 30 (1954) 683-696.

7 1955

J. HEUSCHEN (éd.), *La formation des évangiles. Problème synoptique et Formgeschichte.*
(Recherches Bibliques, 2), Brugge, 1957, 222 p.

J. HEUSCHEN (Luik), Avant-propos   7
J. HEUSCHEN, La formation des évangiles   11-23
L. CERFAUX (Louvain), En marge de la question synoptique.
Les unités littéraires antérieures aux trois premiers évan-
giles [1]   24-33
J. LEVIE (Heverlee), Critique littéraire évangélique et évangile
araméen de l'apôtre Matthieu   34-69
J.W. DOEVE (Holwierde), Le rôle de la tradition orale dans la
composition des Évangiles synoptiques   70-84
X. LÉON-DUFOUR (Lyon-Fourvière), L'épisode de l'enfant
épileptique [2]   85-115
N. VAN BOHEMEN (Weert), L'institution des Douze. Contribution à l'étude des relations entre l'évangile de Matthieu et
celui de Marc   116-151
A. DESCAMPS (Louvain), Du discours de Marc., IX, 33-50 aux
paroles de Jésus   152-177
W.C. VAN UNNIK (Utrecht), L'usage de σῴζειν, «sauver», et
des dérivés dans les évangiles synoptiques [3]   178-194
J. CAMBIER (Heverlee), Historicité des évangiles synoptiques
et Formgeschichte   195-212
B. DE SOLAGES (Toulouse), Note sur l'utilisation de l'analyse
combinatoire pour la solution du problème synoptique .   213-214
B. RIGAUX (Bruxelles), Conclusions. Mise au point pratique
des débats sur le problème synoptique [4]   215-222

1. *Recueil Lucien Cerfaux*, III (BETL, 18), Gembloux, 1962; nouvelle édition revue et complétée (BETL, 71), Leuven, 1985, 99-110.
2. *Études d'évangile*, Paris, 1965, 183-227.
3. *Sparsa Collecta. The Collected Essays of W.C. van Unnik*, I (SupplNT, 29). Leiden, 1973, 16-34.
4. *ETL* 31 (1955) 638-664.

8 1956 ix. 3-5

F.-M. BRAUN (éd.), *L'évangile de Jean. Études et problèmes.*
(Recherches Bibliques, 3), Brugge, 1958, 258 p.

F.-M. BRAUN (Fribourg-en-Suisse), Avant-propos 9
P.-H. MENOUD (Neuchâtel), Les études johanniques de Bult-
mann à Barrett[1] 11-40
M.-É. BOISMARD (Jerusalem), Importance de la critique tex-
tuelle pour établir l'origine araméenne du quatrième
évangile 41-57
V. MARTIN (Genève), Un nouveau Codex de papyrus du IVe
évangile[2] 59-60
H. VAN DEN BUSSCHE (Gent), La structure de Jean I–XII . 61-109
J. GIBLET (Mechelen), Jésus et le «Père» dans le IVe Évangile 111-130
W. GROSSOUW (Nijmegen), La glorification du Christ dans le
quatrième évangile 131-145
L. CERFAUX (Louvain), L'Évangile de Jean et «le logion
johannique» des Synoptiques[3] 147-159
I. DE LA POTTERIE (Leuven), L'impeccabilité du chrétien
d'après I Joh., 3, 6-9[4] 161-177
F.-M. BRAUN, L'arrière-fond du quatrième Évangile . . . 179-196
G. QUISPEL (Utrecht), L'Évangile de Jean et la Gnose . . 197-208
J. COPPENS (Leuven), Le don de l'Esprit d'après les textes de
Qumrân et le quatrième Évangile 209-223
A. LAURENTIN (Paris), Jean, XVII, 5 et la prédestination du
Christ à la gloire chez S. Augustin et ses prédécesseurs . 225-248
F.-M. BRAUN, Conclusions[5] 249-258

1. *Jésus-Christ et la foi. Recherches néotestamentaires* (Bibliothèque théologique),
Neuchâtel-Paris, 1975, 175-199.
2. *ETL* 43 (1956) 547-548.
3. *Recueil Lucien Cerfaux*, III; nouvelle édition (BETL, 71), Leuven, 1985, 161-174.
4. *La vie selon l'esprit. Condition du chrétien* (Unam Sanctam, 55), Paris, 1965, 197-216.
5. *Où en est l'étude du quatrième évangile?*, in *ETL* 32 (1956) 535-546.

9 1957   ix. 5-7

J. VAN DER PLOEG (éd.), *La secte de Qumrân et les origines du christianisme.*
(Recherches Bibliques, 4), Brugge, 1959, 244 p.

J. VAN DER PLOEG (Nijmegen), Avant-propos   9-10
J. VAN DER PLOEG, Six années d'études des manuscrits du Désert
   de Juda (1952-1958)   11-84
G. LAMBERT (Heverlee), Une «Genèse apocryphe» trouvée à
   Qumrân   85-107
J. COPPENS (Leuven), Allusions historiques dans la Genèse
   apocryphe   109-112
A. JAUBERT (Paris), Aperçus sur le calendrier de Qumrân . .   113-120
A.S. VAN DER WOUDE (Noordlaren), Le Maître de Justice et les
   deux Messies de la communauté de Qumrân   121-134
F. NÖTSCHER (Bonn), Voies divines et humaines selon la Bible et
   Qumrân   135-148
J. COPPENS, La piété des psalmistes à Qumrân   149-161
O. BETZ (Tübingen), Le ministère dans la Secte de Qumrân et
   dans le christianisme primitif[1]   162-202
D. BARTHÉLEMY (Fribourg-en-Suisse), La sainteté selon la
   communauté de Qumrân et selon l'Évangile   203-216
J. SCHMITT (Strasbourg), L'organisation de l'Église primitive et
   Qumrân   217-231
L. CERFAUX (Louvain), Influence de Qumrân sur le Nouveau
   Testament[2]   233-244

1. *Der heilige Dienst in der Qumrangemeinde und bei den ersten Christen*, in O. BETZ,
Jesus, der Herr der Kirche. Aufsätze zur biblischen Theologie II (WUNT, 52), Tübingen, 1990,
3-20.

2. *Recueil Lucien Cerfaux*, III; nouvelle édition (BETL, 71), Leuven, 1985, 33-45.

10 1958   viii. 25-30

J. COPPENS, A. DESCAMPS & É. MASSAUX (éd.), *Sacra Pagina. Miscellanea biblica congressus internationalis catholici de re biblica.* (BETL, 12-13), 2 vol., Gembloux, 1959, 579-486 p.

VOLUME I

Préliminaires - Inleidend deel

Patronage et Comité du Congrès. – Hoge Bescherming en Comité   7-8
Rapport sur le Congrès. – Verslag over het Congres   9-13
J.-E. Kardinaal VAN ROEY (Mechelen), Allocution. – Toespraak   14-16
J. COPPENS (Leuven), Allocution. – Toespraak   18-27
R. DE LANGHE (Leuven), Les recherches bibliques à l'Université de Louvain   28-40
L.-T. LEFORT (Louvain), Les recherches orientalistes à l'Université de Louvain   41-49
H. VAN WAEYENBERGH, Recteur Magnifique, Allocution – Toespraak   50-51
Réception des Congressistes à Gand et à Bruges, le 28 août 1958. – Ontvangst van de Congressisten te Gent en te Brugge, op 28 augustus 1958   52-61

I. *Problèmes d'Introduction et d'Herméneutique*
Inleiding tot de Heilige Schrift en Hermeneutiek

B. ALFRINK (aartsbisschop van Utrecht), La vulgarisation de la science biblique et les documents de l'Église   65-75
A.-M. CHARUE (évêque de Namur), Ce que l'Église attend des exégètes   76-85
P. BENOIT (Jerusalem), Les analogies de l'inspiration[1] . . .   86-99
J. LEVIE (Heverlee), Interprétation scripturaire: en exégèse – en théologie   100-118
J. SCHILDENBERGER (Beuron), Aussageabsicht der inspirierten Geschichtsschreiber des Alten Testamentes bei der Kompilation von Überlieferungen, sich widersprechenden Doppelberichten und ätiologischen Erzählungen   119-131
A. DESCAMPS (Louvain), Réflexions sur la méthode en théologie biblique[2]   132-157
M. PEINADOR (Madrid), La integración de la exégesis en la teología. Hacia una auténtica «teología bíblica» . . .   158-179

J.-B. BAUER (Graz), Exégèse patristique, créatrice des symboles[3]   180-186

J. JOMIER (Cairo), L'exégèse coranique actuelle dans le monde arabe   187-193

É. MASSAUX (Louvain), Le papyrus Bodmer II (P 66) et la critique néo-testamentaire   194-207

A. GIL ULECIA (Madrid), Un intéressant lectionnaire latin gothique inconnu. Une contribution à l'étude du texte biblique   208-215

II. *Milieu de l'Ancien Testament*
Oudtestamentisch Milieu

B. VAN DE WALLE (Liège), Le «dieu primordial» chez les Égyptiens   219-228

É. DRIOTON (Paris), Le livre des Proverbes et la Sagesse d'Aménémopé   229-241

G. GOOSSENS (Bruxelles), La philosophie de l'histoire dans l'Ancien Orient   242-252

J. HENNINGER (Fribourg-en-Suisse), Le problème du totémisme chez les Sémites   253-258

R. LARGEMENT (Paris) & H. LEMAITRE (Québec), Le Jour de Yahweh dans le contexte oriental   259-266

M. DAHOOD (Roma), The Linguistic Position of Ugaritic in the Light of Recent Discoveries   267-279

J. DE MENASCE (Paris), Les religions de l'Iran et l'Ancien Testament   280-297

J. PIRENNE (Paris), La religion de Hiérapolis de Syrie au début de notre ère à la lumière des documents récemment exhumés à Hatra   288-299

III. *Exégèse et Théologie de l'Ancien Testament*
Oudtestamentische Exegese en Theologie

A. GELIN (Lyon), La question des «relectures» bibliques à l'intérieur d'une tradition vivante   303-315

P.-P. SAYDON (Malta), Literary Criticism of the Old Testament. Old Problems and New Ways of Solution   316-324

H. GROSS (Trier), «Motivtransposition» als überlieferungsgeschichtliches Prinzip im Alten Testament   325-334

H. HAAG (Luzern), Erwägungen über Beer-Šeba[4]   335-345

L. ARNALDICH (Salamanca), La creación de Eva. Gen., I, 26-27; II, 18-25   346-357

C. HAURET (Strasbourg), Réflexions pessimistes et optimistes sur Gen., IV, 17-24   358-365

A. CHARBEL (Sâo Paulo), Virtus sanguinis non expiatoria in sacrificio šᵉlāmîm 366-376

C. BREKELMANS (Oudenbosch), Le Herem chez les Prophètes du Royaume du Nord et dans le Deutéronome 377-383

A.-M. BRUNET (Montréal), La théologie du Chroniste. Théocratie et messianisme 384-397

H. RENARD (Lille), Le messianisme dans la première partie du livre d'Isaïe 398-407

G. DUNCKER (Roma), «Ut sciat reprobare malum et eligere bonum» (Is., VII, 15b) 408-412

E.-J. KISSANE (Maynooth), The Qumrân Text of Isaiah, IX, 7-9 (1QIsᵃ) 413-418

R. KOCH (Matran, Suisse), La théologie de l'Esprit de Yahvé dans le livre d'Isaïe 419-433

J. COPPENS (Leuven), Le Serviteur de Yahvé. Vers la solution d'une énigme 434-454

B.N. WAMBACQ (Roma), L'unité littéraire de Bar., I–III, 8 . . 455-460

P. AUVRAY (Montsoult, France), Remarques sur la langue d'Ézéchiel 461-470

E. VOGT (Roma), Textumdeutungen im Buch Ezechiel . . . 471-494

A. DEISSLER (Freiburg i. Br.), Der anthologische Charakter des Ps. XLVIII (XLVII) 495-503

J. HOFBAUER (Innsbruck), Ps. LXXXVIII (LXXXIX). Sein Aufbau, seine Herkunft und seine Stellung in der Theologie des Alten Testamentes 504-510

H. CAZELLES (Paris), L'enfantement de la Sagesse en Prov., VIII 511-515

V. HAMP (München), Monotheismus im Alten Testament . . 516-521

A.-M. DUBARLE (Le Saulchoir). La conception de l'homme dans l'Ancien Testament 522-536

J. DE FRAINE (Leuven), Peut-on parler d'un véritable sacerdoce du roi en Israël? 537-547

H. JUNKER (Trier), Segen als heilsgeschichtliches Motivwort im Alten Testament 548-558

O. GARCIA DE LA FUENTE (El Escorial), Sobre la idea de contrición en el Antiguo Testamento 559-579

VOLUME II

IV. *Milieu du Nouveau Testament*
Nieuwtestamentisch Milieu

R. BUSA (Gallarate, Italia), All Non Biblical Dead Sea Scrolls Published up to December 1957 Indexed 7-12

J. VAN DER PLOEG (Nijmegen), La composition littéraire de la «Règle de la Guerre» de Qumrân 13-19

J. MEJÍA (Buenos-Aires), Contribución de Qumrân a la exégesis de los libros de los Macabeos   20-27

J. GAUBET ITURBE (El Escorial), Jerusalén y el Templo del Señor en los manuscritos de Qumrân y en el Nuevo Testamento   28-46

G. BERNINI (Roma), Il giardiniere della piantagione eterna (1QH, VIII)   47-59

R.E. MURPHY (Washington, D.C.), Bśr in the Qumrân Literature and Sarks in the Epistle to the Romans   60-76

Y. JANSSENS (Charleroi), L'épisode de la Samaritaine chez Héracléon   77-85

J. RUYSSCHAERT (Città del Vaticano), Trois campagnes de fouilles au Vatican et la tombe de Pierre   86-97

V. *Exégèse et Théologie du Nouveau Testament*
Nieuwtestamentische Exegese en Theologie

F. GILS (Louvain), Le secret messianique dans les évangiles. Examen de la théorie de E. Sjöberg   101-120

S. MUÑOZ IGLESIAS (Madrid), El evangelio de la infancia en S. Mateo[5]   121-149

J. DUPONT (Bruges), «Soyez parfaits» (Mt., V, 48) − «Soyez miséricordieux» (Lc., VI, 36)   150-162

A. GEORGE (Lyon), Le sens de la parabole des semailles (Mc., IV, 3-9 et parallèles)   163-169

A. HOUSSIAU (Louvain), Le milieu théologique de la leçon εγεννηθη (Jo., I, 13)   170-188

M.-É. BOISMARD (Jerusalem), Le caractère adventice de Jo., XII, 45-50   189-192

I. DE LA POTTERIE (Louvain), La notion de témoignage dans saint Jean[6]   193-208

D. MOLLAT (Chantilly), Le semeion johannique[7]   209-218

S. DE AUSEJO (Sevilla), El concepto de «carne» aplicado a Cristo en el IV evangelio   219-234

R. SCHNACKENBURG (Würzburg), Die Sakramente im Johannesevangelium   235-254

P. FRANQUESA (Tarragona), Influencias ambientales en el Evangelio de S. Juan   255-268

F.-M. BRAUN (Fribourg-en-Suisse), Le quatrième évangile dans l'Église du second siècle   269-279

A. VÖGTLE (Freiburg i. Br.), Ekklesiologische Auftragsworte des Auferstandenen[8]   280-294

A. KERRIGAN (Roma), The «sensus plenior» of Joel, III, 1-5 in Act., II, 14-36   295-313

J.-É. Ménard (Montréal), Le titre ΠΑΙΣ ΘΕΟΥ dans les
Actes des Apôtres 314-321

J.-Mª. Gonzalez Ruiz (Malaga), Sentido comunitario-ecle-
sial de algunos sustantivos abstractos en San Pablo . . 322-341

S. Lyonnet (Roma), La notion de justice de Dieu en Rom.,
III, 5 et l'exégèse paulinienne du «Miserere» 342-356

K.H. Schelkle (Tübingen), Biblische und patristische Eschatologie nach Rom., XIII, 11-13[9] 357-372

L. Cerfaux (Louvain), L'influence des «Mystères» sur les
épîtres de S. Paul aux Colossiens et aux Éphésiens[10] . . 373-379

B. Rigaux (Bruxelles), Vocabulaire chrétien antérieur à la
première épître aux Thessaloniciens 380-389

S. Lach (Lublin), Les ordonnances du culte israélite dans la
lettre aux Hébreux 390-403

P. Bläser (Paderborn), «Lebendigmachender Geist». Ein
Beitrag zur Frage nach den Quellen der paulinischen
Theologie 404-413

A. Feuillet (Paris), Le chapitre X de l'Apocalypse. Son
apport dans la solution du problème eschatologique . 414-429

J. Duplacy (Lyon), D'où vient l'importance centrale de la foi
dans le Nouveau Testament? 430-439

C. Spicq (Fribourg-en-Suisse), Les composantes de la notion
d'*agapè* dans le Nouveau Testament 440-455

B. Capelle (Louvain), Fondements scripturaires de l'angélo-
logie liturgique 456-463

1. *Exégèse et théologie*, III (Cogitatio fidei, 30), Paris, 1968, 17-30.
2. *Überlegungen zur Methode der biblischen Theologie*, in G. Strecker (éd.), *Das Problem der Theologie des Neuen Testaments* (Wege der Forschung, 367). Darmstadt, 1975, 345-377; *Jésus et l'Église. Études d'exégèse et de théologie* (BETL, 77), Leuven, 1987, 1-26.
3. *Scholia Biblica et Patristica*, Graz, 1972, 247-266.
4. *Das Buch des Bundes. Aufsätze zur Bibel und zu ihrer Welt* (ed. B. Lang) (Kommentare und Beiträge zum Alten und Neuen Testament), Düsseldorf, 1980, 37-45.
5. *Estudios biblicos* 17 (1958) 243-273.
6. *El concepto de testimonio en San Juan*, in Id., *La verdad de Jesús. Estudios de cristología joanea* (Biblioteca de Autores Cristianos, 405), Madrid, 1979, 269-283.
7. *Études johanniques* (Parole de Dieu), Paris, 1979, 91-101.
8. *Das Evangelium und die Evangelien. Beiträge zur Evangelienforschung*, Düsseldorf, 1971, 243-252.
9. *Wort und Schrift. Beiträge zur Auslegungsgeschichte des Neuen Testaments*, Düsseldorf, 1966, 239-250.
10. *Recueil Lucien Cerfaux*, III; nouvelle édition (BETL, 71), Leuven, 1985, 279-285.

11 1959   viii. 24-26

A. DESCAMPS (éd.), *Littérature et théologie pauliniennes.*
(Recherches Bibliques, 5), Brugge, 1960, 235 p.

A. DESCAMPS (Louvain), Avant-propos   9-10
A. DESCAMPS, L'actualité de l'épître aux Romains   11-16
B. RIGAUX (Louvain), L'interprétation du paulinisme dans
    l'exégèse récente   17-46
H. RIESENFELD (Uppsala), Le langage parabolique dans les
    épîtres de saint Paul[1]   47-59
L. CERFAUX (Louvain), En faveur de l'authenticité des épîtres
    de la captivité. Homogénéité doctrinale entre Éphésiens
    et les grandes épîtres[2]   60-71
J. CAMBIER (Léopoldville), Connaissance charnelle et spiri-
    tuelle du Christ dans 2 Co 5 16   72-92
L.A. ROOD (Grave), Le Christ comme ΔΥΝΑΜΙΣ ΘΕΟΥ .   93-108
W.C. VAN UNNIK (Utrecht), La conception paulinienne de la
    nouvelle alliance[3]   109-126
H. SCHLIER (Bonn), La notion paulinienne de la parole de
    Dieu   127-141
J. COPPENS (Leuven), Le «mystère» dans la théologie pauli-
    nienne et ses parallèles qumrâniens   142-165
S. LYONNET (Roma), Justification, jugement, rédemption,
    principalement dans l'épître aux Romains   166-184
J. HAVET (Namur), La doctrine paulinienne du «Corps du
    Christ». Essai de mise au point   185-216
M. TESTUZ (Genève), La correspondance apocryphe de saint
    Paul et des Corinthiens   217-223
H. VAN DEN BUSSCHE (Gent-Leuven), Comment enseigner
    saint Paul au séminaire   224-229
A. DESCAMPS, Conclusions   230-235

---

1. *Parabolic Language in the Pauline Epistles*, in *The Gospel Tradition*, Philadelphia,
1970, 187-204.
2. *Recueil Lucien Cerfaux*, III; nouvelle édition (BETL, 71), Leuven, 1985, 265-278.
3. *Sparsa Collecta*, I, 1973, 174-193.

12 1960 viii. 29-31

R. DE LANGHE (éd.), *Le Psautier. Ses origines. Ses problèmes littéraires. Son influence.*
(Orientalia et Biblica Lovaniensia, 4), Leuven, 1962, VI-453 p.

R. DE LANGHE (Leuven), Avant-propos . . . . V-VI
J. COPPENS (Leuven), Les études récentes sur le Psautier . . 1-71
A. DESCAMPS (Louvain), Les genres littéraires du Psautier.
Un état de la question 73-88
J. DE FRAINE (Leuven), «Entmythologisierung» dans les
Psaumes 89-106
A. ARENS (Trier), Hat der Psalter seinen «Sitz im Leben» in
der synagogalen Leseordnung des Pentateuch? . . . 107-131
E. LIPINSKI (Louvain), Les psaumes de la royauté de Yahwé
dans l'exégèse moderne 133-272
P. VAN DEN BERGHE (Leuven), ʿAni et ʿAnaw dans les
psaumes 273-295
A. ROSE, L'influence des psaumes sur les annonces et les
récits de la Passion et de la Résurrection dans les Évan-
giles 297-356
J. DUPONT (Bruges), L'interprétation des psaumes dans les
Actes des Apôtres[1] 357-388
M. BAILLET (Jerusalem), Psaumes, hymnes, cantiques et priè-
res dans les manuscrits de Qumrân 389-405
M. DELCOR (Toulouse), Le Docteur de Justice, nouveau
Moïse, dans les hymnes de Qumrân 407-423
M. MARTIN (Roma), The Babylonian Tradition and Targum 425-451

1. *Études sur les Actes des Apôtres* (Lectio Divina, 45), Paris, 1967, 283-307; = *The Salvation of the Gentiles. Essays on the Acts of the Apostles*, New York-Ramsay-Toronto, 1979, 103-128.

13 1961

É. Massaux (éd.), *La venue du Messie. Messianisme et eschatologie.*
(Recherches Bibliques, 6), Brugge, 1962, 260 p.

É. Massaux (Louvain), Avant-propos 9-17
P. Grelot (Paris), Le Messie dans les Apocryphes de l'Ancien Testament. État de la question 19-50
H. Riesenfeld (Uppsala), Le caractère messianique de la tentation au désert[1] 51-63
M. Sabbe (Brugge), La rédaction du récit de la Transfiguration[2]. 65-100
J. Coppens (Leuven), Le Messianisme sacerdotal dans les écrits du Nouveau Testament 101-112
B. van Iersel (Nijmegen), Fils de David et Fils de Dieu . 113-132
F.-M. Braun (Fribourg-en-Suisse), Messie, Logos et Fils de l'homme 133-147
A. Feuillet (Paris), Le triomphe du Fils de l'homme d'après la déclaration du Christ aux Sanhédrites (Mc., XIV, 62; Mt., XXVI, 64; Lc., XXII, 69) 149-171
B. Rigaux (Louvain), La seconde venue de Jésus 173-216
H. Quecke (Heidelberg), L'Évangile de Thomas. État des recherches 217-241
L. Leloir (Clervaux), Le Diatessaron de Tatien et son commentaire par Éphrem 243-260

1. *The Messianic Character of the Temptation in the Wilderness,* in *The Gospel Tradition,* 1970, 75-93.
2. *Studia Neotestamentica* (BETL, 98), Leuven, 1991, 65-100.

14 1962

J. GIBLET (éd.), *Aux origines de l'Église.*
(Recherches Bibliques, 7), Brugge, 1965, 199 p.[1]

J. GIBLET (Louvain), Avant-propos 9-12
J. COPPENS (Leuven), L'Église, nouvelle alliance de Dieu avec
   son peuple 13-22
A.-M. DENIS (Huy), Évolution de structures dans la secte de
   Qumrân 23-49
J. GIBLET, Les Douze. Histoire et théologie 51-64
H. VAN DEN BUSSCHE (Leuven), L'Église dans le quatrième
   Évangile 65-85
P. ANDRIESSEN (Egmond), La nouvelle Ève, corps du nouvel
   Adam 87-109
L. CERFAUX (Louvain), L'Église dans l'Apocalypse . . . 111-124
J. COPPENS (Leuven), L'eucharistie. Sacrement et sacrifice de
   la nouvelle alliance. Fondement de l'Église 125-158
P. GRELOT (Paris), La vocation ministérielle au service du
   peuple de Dieu 159-173
W.C. VAN UNNIK (Utrecht), Les idées des gnostiques concer-
   nant l'Église[2] 175-187
R. MARLÉ (Paris), L'Église dans l'exégèse et la théologie de
   Bultmann 189-199

1. *Vom Christus zur Kirche. Charisma und Amt im Urchristentum*, Wien, 1966, 251 p.;
The Birth of the Church. A Biblical Study. Translated by C.U. QUINN, Staten Island NY,
1968, 255 p.
2. *Sparsa Collecta*, III (SupplNT, 31), Leiden, 1983, 285-296.

15 1963

C. HAURET (éd.), *Aux grands carrefours de la révélation et de l'exégèse de l'Ancien Testament.*
(Recherches Bibliques, 8), Brugge, 1967, 191 p.

C. HAURET (Strasbourg), Avant-propos   11-12
D. BARTHÉLEMY (Fribourg-en-Suisse), La place de la Septante dans l'Église   13-28
H. CAZELLES (Paris), Laban change dix fois le salaire de Jacob   29-34
T. VRIEZEN (Utrecht), Exode, XX, 2. Introduction au Décalogue: formule de loi ou d'alliance   35-50
G. MINETTE DE TILLESSE (Orval), Martin Noth et la Redaktionsgeschichte des Livres historiques   51-75
C.H.W. BREKELMANS (Nijmegen), Éléments deutéronomiques dans le Pentateuque   77-91
H. GROSS (Trier), Le prétendu «ministère prophétique» en Israël[1]   93-105
A. SCHOORS (Leuven), L'eschatologie dans les prophéties du Deutéro-Isaïe   107-128
C. HAURET, Les ennemis-sorciers dans les supplications individuelles   129-137
A.-M. DUBARLE (Le Saulchoir), Le Cantique des Cantiques dans l'exégèse récente   139-152
J. COPPENS (Leuven), Le Pré-messianisme vétérotestamentaire   153-179
R. DE LANGHE (Leuven), Ras Shamra-Ugarit depuis 1945 .   181-191

1. *Gab es in Israel ein «Prophetisches Amt»?*, in *ETL* 41 (1965) 5-19.

16 1965

I. DE LA POTTERIE (éd.), *De Jésus aux évangiles. Tradition et rédaction dans les évangiles synoptiques.* Donum natalicium J. Coppens, vol. II. (BETL, 25), Gembloux, 1967, 271 p.[1]

I. DE LA POTTERIE (Roma), Préface . . . .   VII-XIV
X. LÉON-DUFOUR (Lyon-Fourvière), Interprétation des Évangiles et problème synoptique[2]   5-16
S. McLOUGHLIN (Douai Abbey), Les accords mineurs Mt-Lc contre Mc et le problème synoptique. Vers la théorie des deux sources[3]   17-40
F. NEIRYNCK (Leuven), La rédaction matthéenne et la structure du premier Évangile[4]   41-73
J. DELORME (Lyon), Aspects doctrinaux du second Évangile. Études récentes de la rédaction de Marc[5]   74-99
A. GEORGE (Lyon), Tradition et rédaction chez Luc. La construction du troisième Évangile[6]   100-129
P. BONNARD (Lausanne), Composition et signification historique de Matthieu, XVIII[7]   130-140
J. LAMBRECHT (Heverlee), La structure de Mc., XIII[8] . .   141-164
E. RASCO (Roma), Les paraboles de Luc, XV. Une invitation à la joie de Dieu dans le Christ   165-183
M. SABBE (Brugge), Le baptême de Jésus[9].   184-211
B.M.F. VAN IERSEL (Nijmegen), La vocation de Lévi (Mc., II, 13-17; Mt., IX, 9-13; Lc., V, 27-32). Tradition et rédactions   212-232
A.-M. DENIS (Louvain), La marche de Jésus sur les eaux. Contribution à l'histoire de la péricope dans la tradition évangélique   233-247
M. DIDIER (Namur), La parabole des talents et des mines .   248-271

1. *Da Gesù ai Vangeli. Tradizione e redazione nei vangeli sinottici*, Assisi, 1971, 339 p.
2. *ETL* 43 (1967) 5-16.
3. *Ibid.*, 17-40.
4. *Ibid.*, 41-73; *Evangelica* (BETL, 60), Leuven, 1982, 3-35.
5. *ETL* 43 (1967) 74-99.
6. *Ibid.*, 100-129; *Études sur l'œuvre de Luc* (Sources bibliques), Paris, 1978, 15-41.
7. *Anamnesis. Recherches sur le Nouveau Testament* (Cahiers de la Revue de théologie et de philosophie, 3), Genève, 1980, 111-120.
8. *Die Redaktion der Markus-Apokalypse* (Analecta biblica, 28), Roma, 1967, 261-297: «Mk 13: Die Struktur».
9. *Studia Neotestamentica* (BETL, 98), 105-132.

17 1966

G. THILS & R.E. BROWN (éd.), *Exégèse et théologie.*
Donum natalicium J. Coppens, vol. III.
(BETL, 26), Gembloux, 1968, 328 p.

G. THILS (Louvain), Préface . . . .   VII-X
G. VAN RIET (Louvain), Exégèse et réflexion philosophique [1]   1-16
P. ASVELD (Graz), Exégèse critique et exégèse dogmatique [2] .   17-31
P. GRELOT (Paris), Que penser de l'interprétation existen-
tiale? [3]   32-55
J. CAHILL (Chicago), Death of God Theology as Biblical
Hermeneutic [4]   56-71
R.E. BROWN (Baltimore), The Problems of the Sensus Ple-
nior [5]   72-81
M.L. RAMLOT (Toulouse), Histoire et mentalité symbolique   82-190
A. VÖGTLE (Freiburg i. Br.), Die hermeneutische Relevanz
des geschichtlichen Charakters der Christusoffenbarung [6]   191-208
L. MALEVEZ (Louvain), Le Christ et la foi   209-246
S. TROOSTER (Maastricht), L'Eucharistie, approche théolo-
gique   247-261
J. COPPENS (Leuven), L'Eucharistie néo-testamentaire . .   262-281
Subsidia bibliographica:
J. COPPENS, L'herméneutique biblique. Introduction biblio-
graphique   282-315
U. SCHEIRE (Leuven), L'œuvre de Henri Duméry. Relevé
bibliographique   315-327

1. *ETL* 43 (1967) 389-404.
2. *Ibid.*, 405-419.
3. *Ibid.*, 420-443.
4. *Ibid.*, 444-459.
5. *Ibid.*, 460-469.
6. *Ibid.*, 470-487; *Das Evangelium und die Evangelien. Beiträge zur Evangelienforschung*, Düsseldorf, 1971, 16-30.

18 1967

H. CAZELLES (éd.), *De Mari à Qumrân. L'Ancien Testament et son milieu.*
Donum natalicium J. Coppens, vol. I.
(BETL, 24), Gembloux, 1969, 370 p.

I
HOMMAGE DES JOURNÉES BIBLIQUES À MGR J. COPPENS [1]

Lettre de S. Ém. le cardinal Suenens 7*
A. SCHOORS (Leuven), Het wetenschappelijk werk van Monseigneur Coppens 9*-28*
A. SCHOORS, L'œuvre scientifique de Monseigneur Coppens   29*-49*
G. RYCKMANS, Monseigneur Joseph Coppens. Notes d'un témoin 51*-65*
G. THILS (Louvain), Allocution – Toespraak 67*-69*
L. VAN PETEGHEM (bisschop van Gent), Toespraak – Allocution 71*-74*
A. DESCAMPS (recteur magnifique de l'Université catholique de Louvain), Allocution – Toespraak 75*-80*
A. CHARUE (évêque de Namur), Toast au diner du 25 août 1967 . . . .   81*-82*
Réponse de Mgr Coppens – Antwoord van Mgr. Coppens   83*-93*
Bibliographia Academica J. Coppens 95*-132*
Tabula gratulatoria 133*-158*

II
L'ANCIEN TESTAMENT
SON MILIEU. SES ÉCRITS. SES RELECTURES JUIVES

A. PETITJEAN – J. COPPENS (Louvain-Leuven), Mari et l'Ancien Testament   3-13
M. DAHOOD (Rome), Ugaritic and the Old Testament [2] . .   14-33
H. CAZELLES (Paris), Positions actuelles dans l'exégèse du Pentateuque [3]   34-57
J. SCHARBERT (München), Die prophetische Literatur. Der Stand der Forschung [4]   58-118
D. WINTON THOMAS (Cambridge), A Consideration of Isaiah LIII in the Light of Recent Textual and Philological Study [5]   119-126
J. LUST (Brugge), Éz., XX, 4-26. Une parodie de l'histoire religieuse d'Israël [6]   127-166
J. LUST, «Mon Seigneur Jahweh» dans le texte hébreu d'Ézéchiel [7]   167-173

J. VAN DER PLOEG (Nijmegen), L'étude du Psautier 1960-1967   174-191

J. ANGÉNIEUX (Beyrouth), Le Cantique des Cantiques en huit chants à refrains alternants[8]   192-245

A.-M. DUBARLE (Le Saulchoir), Où en est l'étude de la littérature sapientielle?[9]   246-258

E. JACOB (Strasbourg), La théologie de l'Ancien Testament. État présent et perspectives d'avenir[10]   259-271

H.H. ROWLEY (Manchester), L'histoire de la secte qumrânienne   272-301

R. LE DÉAUT (Roma), Les études targumiques. État de la recherche et perspectives pour l'exégèse de l'Ancien Testament[11]   302-331

1. *La carrière et l'œuvre scientifique d'un maître louvaniste. Hommage - Hulde J. Coppens 1927-1967* (ALBO, IV/49), Leuven, 1969, 158 p.
2. *ETL* 44 (1968) 35-54.
3. *Ibid.*, 55-78.
4. *Ibid.*, 346-406.
5. *Ibid.*, 79-86.
6. *ETL* 43 (1967) 488-527.
7. *ETL* 44 (1968) 482-488.
8. *Ibid.*, 87-140.
9. *Ibid.*, 407-419.
10. *Ibid.*, 259-271.
11. *Ibid.*, 5-34.

19 1968

F. NEIRYNCK (éd.), *L'évangile de Luc. Problèmes littéraires et théologiques. Mémorial Lucien Cerfaux.*
(BETL, 32), Gembloux, 1973, 385 p.; nouvelle édition augmentée, Leuven, 1989.

I

A. DESCAMPS (Louvain), Monseigneur Lucien Cerfaux. Ébauche d'un portrait[1]   9-21

J. COPPENS (Leuven), La carrière et l'œuvre scientifiques de Monseigneur Lucien Cerfaux[2]   23-59

L. CERFAUX, L'utilisation de la Source Q par Luc. Introduction du séminaire   61-69
        [2]1989, 285-293

Bibliographie Lucien Cerfaux[3]   71-90

II

W.G. KÜMMEL (Marburg), Luc en accusation dans la théologie contemporaine[4]   93-109
        [2]1989, 3-19, 295

J. DUPLACY (Dijon), P[75] (Pap. Bodmer XIV-XV) et les formes les plus anciennes du texte de Luc[5]   111-128
        [2]1989, 21-38, 295

W.C. VAN UNNIK (Utrecht), Éléments artistiques dans l'évangile de Luc[6]   129-140
        [2]1989, 39-50, 295

E.E. ELLIS (New Brunswick, NJ), La fonction de l'eschatologie dans l'évangile de Luc[7]   141-155
        [2]1989, 51-65, 296-303

F. NEIRYNCK (Leuven), La matière marcienne dans l'évangile de Luc[8]   157-201
        [2]1989, 67-111, 304-305

J. DELOBEL (Leuven), La rédaction de Lc., IV, 14-16a et le «Bericht vom Anfang»   203-223
        [2]1989, 113-133, 306-312

R. PESCH (Frankfurt), La rédaction lucanienne du logion des pêcheurs d'hommes (Lc., V, 10c)[9]   225-244
        [2]1989, 135-154, 313-315

A. DENAUX (Brugge), L'hypocrisie des Pharisiens et le dessein de Dieu. Analyse de Lc., XIII, 31-33   245-285
        [2]1989, 155-195, 316-323

B. Dehandschutter (Leuven), L'Évangile selon Thomas:
témoin d'une tradition prélucanienne?   287-297
²1989, 197-207, 324-326

É. Samain (Tournai), La notion de APXH dans l'œuvre
lucanienne   299-328
²1989, 209-238, 327

J. Dupont (Ottignies), Les discours de Pierre dans les Actes
et le chapitre XXIV de l'évangile de Luc   329-374
²1989, 239-284, 328-330

1. *ETL* 45 (1969) 45-57; *Recueil L. Cerfaux*, III, nouvelle édition revue et augmentée (BETL, 71), Leuven, 1985, xi-xxiii.

2. *ETL* 45 (1969) 8-44; *Recueil L. Cerfaux*, III, ²1985, xxiv-lx.

3. *Recueil L. Cerfaux*, III, ²1985, lxi-lxxx.

4. *ETL* 46 (1970) 265-281; *Lukas in der Anklage der heutigen Theologie,* in *ZNW* 63 (1972) 149-165; G. Braumann (éd.), *Das Lukas-Evangelium* (Wege der Forschung, 280), Darmstadt, 1974, 416-426; *Heilsgeschehen und Geschichte. Band 2. Gesammelte Aufsätze 1965-1977* (Marburger theologische Studien, 16), Marburg, 1978, 87-100; English translation: *Current Theological Accusations Against Luke*, in *Andover Newton Quarterly Review* 16 (1975) 131-145.

5. *Études de critique textuelle du Nouveau Testament*, éd. J. Delobel (BETL, 78), Leuven, 1987, 151-168.

6. *ETL* 46 (1970) 401-412.

7. *Die Funktion der Eschatologie im Lukasevangelium*, in *ZTK* 66 (1969) 387-402; G. Braumann (éd.), *Das Lukas-Evangelium*, 378-397. In English: *Eschatology in Luke*, Philadelphia, 1972.

8. *Evangelica* (BETL, 60), 37-81.

9. *ETL* 46 (1970) 413-432.

10. *Nouvelles études sur les Actes des Apôtres* (Lectio Divina, 128), Paris, 1984, 58-111.

The Gospel of Luke: Supplement 1989

T.A. Friedrichsen, The Matthew-Luke Agreements against Mark.
A Survey of Recent Studies: 1974-1989   335-391
F. Neirynck – T.A. Friedrichsen, Note on Luke 9,22.
A Response to M.D. Goulder   393-398
C.J. Schreck, The Nazareth Pericope: Luke 4:16-30 in Recent Study   399-471
P.J. Judge, Luke 7,1-10: Sources and Redaction   473-489
J. Verheyden, The Source(s) of Luke 21   491-516
F.J. Matera, Luke 22,66-71: Jesus before the ΠΡΕΣΒΥΤΕΡΙΟΝ   517-533
F.J. Matera, Luke 23,1-25: Jesus before Pilate, Herod and Israel   535-551
G. Bouwman, Le 'premier livre' (Act., I,1) et la date des Actes des Apôtres . .   553-565

20 1969 ix. 3-5

W.C. VAN UNNIK (éd.), *La littérature juive entre Tenach et Mischna. Quelques problèmes.* (Recherches Bibliques, 9), Leiden, 1974, 163 p.

W.C. VAN UNNIK (Utrecht), Quelques problèmes. Leçon d'ouverture 1-14
M. BLACK (St. Andrews), The Fragments of the Aramaic Enoch from Qumran 15-28
K.H. RENGSTORF (Münster), Herkunft und Sinn der Patriarchen-Reden in den Testamenten der zwölf Patriarchen . 29-47
B. DEHANDSCHUTTER (Leuven), Le rêve dans l'Apocryphe de la Genèse 48-55
P.-M. BOGAERT (Maredsous), Le nom de Baruch dans la littérature pseudépigraphique: l'Apocalypse syriaque et le livre deutérocanonique 56-72
M. PHILONENKO (Strasbourg), Joseph et Aséneth: Questions actuelles 73-76
C. BURCHARD (Göttingen), Joseph et Aséneth: Questions actuelles 77-100
M. DELCOR (Toulouse), Le milieu d'origine et le développement de l'apocalyptique juive[1] 101-117
J.W. DOEVE (Utrecht), Le domaine du temple de Jérusalem 118-163

1. *Études bibliques et orientales de religions comparées*, Leiden, 1979, 193-209.

21 1970.   ix. 1-3

M. DIDIER (éd.), *L'évangile selon Matthieu. Rédaction et théologie.*
(BETL, 29), Gembloux, 1972, 428 p.

M. DIDIER (Namur), Journées bibliques de Louvain 1970:
l'Évangile selon Matthieu   11-19

C.M. MARTINI (Roma), La problématique générale du texte
de Matthieu[1]   21-36
F. NEIRYNCK (Leuven), The Gospel of Matthew and Literary
Criticism. A Critical Analysis of A. Gaboury's Hypo-
thesis[2]   37-69
M. DEVISCH (Leuven), Le document Q, source de Matthieu.
Problématique actuelle   71-97
J. SMIT SIBINGA (Amsterdam), Eine literarische Technik im
Matthäusevangelium   99-105
F. VAN SEGBROECK (Leuven), Les citations d'accomplis-
sement dans l'Évangile selon saint Matthieu d'après trois
ouvrages récents   107-130
L. HARTMAN (Uppsala), Scriptural Exegesis in the Gospel of
St. Matthew and the Problem of Communication . .   131-152
A. VÖGTLE (Freiburg i. Br.), Die matthäische Kindheits-
geschichte   153-183
G. STRECKER (Göttingen), Les macarismes du discours sur la
montagne[3]   185-208
K. GATZWEILER (Liège), Les récits de miracles dans l'Évangile
selon saint Matthieu   209-220
J. DUPONT (Ottignies), Le point de vue de Matthieu dans le
chapitre des paraboles[4]   221-259
J. KAHMANN (Heerlen), Die Verheissung an Petrus: Mt.,
XVI, 18-19 im Zusammenhang des Matthäusevange-
liums   261-280
É. COTHENET (Paris), Les prophètes chrétiens dans l'Évangile
selon saint Matthieu   281-308
J. LAMBRECHT (Leuven), The Parousia Discourse. Composi-
tion and Content in Mt., XXIV–XXV   309-342
D. SENIOR (Leuven), The Passion Narrative in the Gospel of
Matthew   343-357

A. DESCAMPS (Louvain), Rédaction et christologie dans le
récit matthéen de la Passion[5] 359-415

S. LÉGASSE (Toulouse), L'«antijudaïsme» dans l'Évangile
selon Matthieu 417-428

1. *La parola di Dio alle origini della Chiesa*, Roma, 1980, 129-145.

2 *SBL Seminar Papers 1972*, I, 147-179; *Evangelica* (BETL, 60), 691-723.

3. *Die Makarismen der Bergpredigt*, in *NTS* 17 (1970-71) 255-275; *Eschaton und Historie. Aufsätze*, Göttingen, 1979, 108-131.

4. *Études sur les Évangiles synoptiques* (BETL, 70), Leuven, 1985, 869-907.

5. *Jésus et l'Église* (BETL, 77), Leuven, 1987, 185-241.

22 1971 viii. 31 - ix. 2

M. SABBE (éd.), *L'évangile selon Marc. Tradition et rédaction.* (BETL, 34), Gembloux-Leuven, 1974, 594 p.; nouvelle édition augmentée, Leuven, 1988, 601 p.

J.M. ROBINSON (Claremont), The Literary Composition of Mark 11-20
E. BEST (St. Andrews), Mark's Preservation of the Tradition [1]   21-34
W. HENDRIKS (Nijmegen), Zur Kollektionsgeschichte des Markusevangeliums 35-57
M. DEVISCH (Leuven), La relation entre l'évangile de Marc et le document Q 59-91
M.-É. BOISMARD (Jérusalem), Influences matthéennes sur l'ultime rédaction de l'évangile de Marc 93-102
F. NEIRYNCK (Leuven), Urmarcus redivivus? Examen critique de l'hypothèse des insertions matthéennes dans Marc [2] 103-146
J. KONINGS (Leuven), The Pre-Markan Sequence in Jn., VI: A Critical Re-examination 147-178
D.L. DUNGAN (Tennessee), Reactionary Trends in the Gospel Producing Activity of the Early Church: Marcion, Tatian, Mark 179-202
B. DEHANDSCHUTTER (Leuven), La parabole des vignerons homicides (Mc., XII, 1-12) et l'Évangile selon Thomas . 203-220
J. RADERMAKERS (Bruxelles), L'évangile de Marc. Structure et théologie 221-239
P. MOURLON BEERNAERT (Bruxelles), Structure littéraire et lecture théologique de Marc 14,17-52 241-268
J. LAMBRECHT (Leuven), Redaction and Theology in Mk., IV   269-308
J.M. VAN CANGH (Louvain), La multiplication des pains dans l'évangile de Marc. Essai d'exégèse globale . . . 309-346
T. SNOY (Louvain), Marc 6,48: «... et il voulait les dépasser». Proposition pour la solution d'une énigme ... 347-363
R. PESCH (Frankfurt), Der Schluß der vormarkinischen Passionsgeschichte und des Markusevangeliums: Mk 15,42–16,8 365-410
H.W. BARTSCH (Frankfurt), Der ursprüngliche Schluß der Leidensgeschichte. Überlieferungsgeschichliche Studien zum Markus-Schluß 411-433

K. ALAND (Münster), Der Schluß der Markusevangeliums[3]   435-470

N. PERRIN (Chicago), The Christology of Mark[4]   471-485

J. COPPENS (Leuven), Les logia du Fils de l'homme dans
l'évangile de Marc[5]   487-528

A. DESCAMPS (Louvain), Pour une histoire du titre «Fils de
Dieu». Les antécédents par rapport à Marc[6]   529-571

Notes additionnelles: E. Best (572-573); K. Aland (573-575).

1. *Markus als Bewahrer der Überlieferung*, in R. PESCH (éd.), *Das Markus-Evangelium* (Wege der Forschung, 411), Darmstadt, 1979, 390-409; *Disciples and Discipleship. Studies in the Gospel according to Mark*, Edinburgh, 1986, 31-48.

2. *Jean et les Synoptiques* (BETL, 49), Leuven, 1979, 319-361.

3. *Neutestamentliche Entwürfe* (Theologische Bücherei, 63), München, 1979, 264-283.

4. *The Journal of Religion* 51 (1971) 173-187; *A Modern Pilgrimage in New Testament Christology*, Philadelphia, 1974, 104-121; *Die Christologie des Markus-Evangeliums*, in R. PESCH (éd.), *Das Markus-Evangelium*, 356-376.

5. *Le Fils de l'homme néotestamentaire* (BETL, 55), Leuven, 1981, 109-149.

6. *Jésus et l'Église* (BETL, 77), Leuven, 1987, 91-133.

Addendum: F. NEIRYNCK, «Duality in Mark and the Limits of Source Criticism» = *Duplicate Expressions in the Gospel of Mark*, in *ETL* 48 (1972) 150-209; *Duality in Mark* (BETL, 31), Leuven, 1972, ²1988, 13-72; *Evangelica* (BETL, 60), 83-142.

23 1972

C. Brekelmans (éd.), *Questions disputées d'Ancien Testament. Méthode et théologie.*
(BETL, 33), Gembloux-Leuven, 1974, 202 p.; revised and enlarged edition by M. Vervenne, Leuven, 1989, 246 p.

C. Brekelmans, Avant-propos de la première édition . . 7
M. Dahood (Roma), Northwest Semitic Texts and Textual
  Criticism of the Hebrew Bible 11-37
J. Barr (Manchester), Philology and Exegesis. Some General
  Remarks, with Illustrations from Job 39-61
J.F.A. Sawyer (Newcastle), The «Original Meaning of the
  Text» and Other Legitimate Subjects for Semantic Des-
  cription 63-70
E. Kutsch (Erlangen), Gottes Zuspruch und Anspruch. Berît
  in der alttestamentlichen Theologie 71-90
D.J. McCarthy (Roma), Covenant-Relationships . . . 91-103
P.A.H. de Boer (Oegstgeest), Quelques remarques sur l'arc
  dans la nuée (Gen. 9,8-17)[1] 105-114
L. Dequeker (Leuven), Noah and Israel. The Everlasting
  Divine Covenant with Mankind 115-129
P. Buis (Rungis), Comment au septième siècle envisageait-on
  l'avenir de l'Alliance? Étude de Lv. 26,3-45 131-140
R. Martin-Achard (Genève), Quelques remarques sur la
  nouvelle alliance chez Jérémie (Jérémie 31,31-34)[2] . . 141-164
H.D. Preuss (Neuendettelsau), Alttestamentliche Weisheit in
  christlicher Theologie? 165-181
J. Lévêque (Paris), Le contrepoint théologique apporté par la
  réflexion sapientielle 183-202
Supplementary Notes 203-222
Indexes 225-246

1. *Selected Studies in Old Testament Exegesis.* Edited by C. van Duin (Oudtestamentische Studiën, 27), Leiden, 1991, 129-138.
2. *Permanence de l'Ancien Testament. Recherches d'exégèse et de théologie* (Cahiers de la Revue de théologie et de philosophie, 11), Genève, 1984, 55-78.

J. DUPONT (éd.), *Jésus aux origines de la christologie.*
(BETL, 40), Gembloux-Leuven, 1975, 375 p.; nouvelle édition
augmentée, Leuven, 1989, 458 p.

J. DUPONT (Ottignies), Introduction: Jésus aux origines de la
christologie[1] 9-22

A.-L. DESCAMPS (Louvain), Portée christologique de la
recherche historique sur Jésus[2] 23-46
E. KÄSEMANN (Tübingen), Die neue Jesus-Frage 47-57
D. LÜHRMANN (Bethel), Die Frage nach Kriterien für ur-
sprüngliche Jesusworte – eine Problemskizze 59-72
J.A. FITZMYER (Cambridge, Mass.), Methodology in the
Study of the Aramaic Substratum of Jesus' Sayings in
the New Testament[3] 73-102
E. LINNEMANN (Braunschweig), Hat Jesus Naherwartung
gehabt? 103-110
P. BENOIT (Jerusalem), Jésus et le Serviteur de Dieu . . . 111-140
X. LÉON-DUFOUR (Lyon-Fourvière), Jésus devant sa mort, à
la lumière des textes de l'Institution eucharistique et des
discours d'adieu 141-168
M. DE JONGE (Leiden), The Use of ὁ χριστός in the Passion
Narratives[4] 169-192
E.E. ELLIS (New Brunswick, N.J.), La composition de Luc 9
et les sources de sa christologie[5] 193-200
M. RESE (Münster), Einige Überlegungen zu Lukas XIII, 31-
33 201-225
F. NEIRYNCK (Leuven), Jésus and the Sabbath. Some Obser-
vations on Mk II,27[6] 227-270
J.B. MUDDIMAN (Oxford), Jesus and Fasting (Mark 2,18-22) 271-281
A. GEORGE (Lyon), Paroles de Jésus sur ses miracles (Mt
11,5.21; 12,27.28 et par.) 283-301
I. DE LA POTTERIE (Rome), Le sens primitif de la multiplica-
tion des pains 303-329
J. DUPONT, Les implications christologiques de la parabole
de la brebis perdue[7] 331-350
J. DUPONT, Conclusion des Journées Bibliques: les énigmes 351-356
de l'histoire de Jésus[8] . . . .
J. LAMBRECHT, Jesus and the Law. An Investigation of Mk
7,1-23[9] 358-416

Notes additionnelles **417-434**

1. *Études sur les Évangiles Synoptiques* (BETL, 70), Leuven, 1985, 3-16.
2. *Jesus et l'Église* (BETL, 77), Leuven, 1987, 27-50.
3. *The Study of the Aramaic Background of the New Testament*, in *A Wandering Aramean. Collected Aramaic Essays* (SBL MS, 25), Missoula, MT, 1979, 1-27.
4. *Jewish Eschatology, Early Christian Christology and the Testaments of the Twelve Patriarchs: Collected Essays* (SupplNT, 63), Leiden, 1991, 63-86.
5. *The Composition of Luke 9 and the Sources of Its Christology*, in G.F. HAWTHORNE (éd.), *Current Issues in Biblical and Patristic Interpretation. Studies in Honor of Merril C. Tenney*, Grand Rapids, MI, 1975, 121-127.
6. *Evangelica* (BETL, 60), 637-680.
7. *Études sur les Évangiles Synoptiques*, 1985, 647-666.
8. *Ibid.*, 17-22.
9. *ETL* 53 (1977) 24-79.

25 1974

J. COPPENS (éd.), *La notion biblique de Dieu. Le Dieu de la Bible et le Dieu des philosophes.*
(BETL, 41), Gembloux-Leuven, 1976; Leuven, ²1985, 519 p.

I
LA JOURNÉE JUBILAIRE DU 27 AOÛT 1974
MESSAGES ET ALLOCUTIONS

J. COPPENS, La journée jubilaire du 27 août 1974[1] 15-20
J. Cardinal VILLOT (Roma), Lettre [à Monseigneur Coppens, président des XXVes Journées bibliques] 21-22
J. COPPENS (Leuven), Vingt-cinq années de Journées Bibliques à Louvain. Un aperçu historique 23-47
B. Kardinaal ALFRINK (Utrecht), Toespraak ter gelegenheid van de 25e bijeenkomst van de Leuvense Bijbel-studiedagen 49-50
H. SERVOTTE (Leuven), Toespraak op de viering van het 25-jarig bestaan van de Leuvense Bijbeldagen 51-52
A. HOUSSIAU (Louvain), Adresse aux organisateurs et participants des 25es Journées Bibliques de Louvain 53-55
B. RIGAUX (Louvain), Adresse au nom des Anciens des Journées Bibliques 57-60

II
LES APPORTS VÉTÉRO- ET INTERTESTAMENTAIRES

J. COPPENS, La notion vétérotestamentaire de Dieu. Position du problème 63-76
H. CAZELLES (Paris), Le Dieu du Yahviste et de l'Élohiste ou le Dieu du Patriarche, de Moïse et de David avant les prophètes 77-89
J. LUST (Leuven), Elijah and the Theophany on Mount Horeb 91-100
N. LOHFINK (Frankfurt a. M.), Gott im Buch Deuteronomium 101-126
W. ZIMMERLI (Göttingen), Gott in der Verkündigung der Propheten 127-143
P.R. ACKROYD (London), God and People in the Chronicler's Presentation of Ezra 145-162
J. COPPENS, Le péché offense de Dieu ou du prochain? Note sur le Ps. LI,6 et Lc., XV,18.21 163-167

A. Barucq (Lyon), Dieu chez les Sages d'Israël   169-189
M. Gilbert (Louvain), La connaissance de Dieu selon le
   Livre de la Sagesse   191-210
M. Delcor (Toulouse), Le Dieu des Apocalypticiens[2] . .   209-228

III
Les apports néo-testamentaires

J. Giblet (Louvain), La révélation de Dieu dans le Nouveau
   Testament. Position du problème   231-244
S. Légasse (Toulouse), Le logion sur le Fils révélateur (Mt.,
   XI, 27 par. Lc., X, 22). Essai d'analyse prérédactionnelle   245-274
E. Schweizer (Zürich), «Pour que Dieu soit tout en tous»
   (I Cor., XV, 28). Contribution à la notion de l'image de
   Dieu dans les perspectives eschatologiques de Jésus et de
   Paul   275-291
K.P. Donfried (Northampton, Mass.), Justification and Last
   Judgment in Paul   293-313
A. Vanhoye (Roma), Le Dieu de la nouvelle alliance dans
   l'épître aux Hébreux   315-330
J. Coppens, Dieu le Père dans la théologie paulinienne . .   331-335
J. Legrand (Bangalore), The Areopagus Speech: Its Theolo-
   gical Kerygma and its Missionary Significance[3] . . .   337-350
P. Bonnard (Lausanne), Contemplation johannique et mys-
   tique hellénistique[4]   351-360
C.K. Barrett (Durham), Christocentric or Theocentric?
   Observations on the Theological Method of the Fourth
   Gospel   361-376
A. Vögtle (Freiburg i. Br.), Der Gott der Apokalypse. Wie
   redet die christliche Apokalypse von Gott?   377-398

IV
Le Dieu de la Bible et le Dieu des Philosophes

A. Gesché (Louvain), Le Dieu de la Bible et la théologie
   spéculative   401-430
J. Van der Veken (Leuven), Can the True God be the God
   of one Book? The Particularity of Religion and the
   Universitality of Reason   431-444

1. *Tafelrede W.C. van Unnick (17-20)*
2. *Études bibliques et orientales de religions comparées*, 1979, 210-227.
3. *God's Word Among Men. Theological Essays in Honor of Joseph Putz*, Delhi, 1974, 59-71.
4. *Anamnesis*, 1980, 177-185.

26 1975   viii. 20-22

M. DE JONGE (éd.), *L'évangile de Jean. Sources, rédaction, théologie.*
(BETL, 44), Gembloux-Leuven, 1977; Leuven, ²1987, 416 p.

M. DE JONGE (Leiden), Introduction   13-18

I

R. SCHNACKENBURG (Würzburg), Entwicklung und Stand der
    johanneischen Forschung seit 1955[1]   19-44
J. GIBLET (Louvain), Développements dans la théologie
    johannique   45-72
F. NEIRYNCK (Leuven), John and the Synoptics[2]   73-106
B. LINDARS (Cambridge), Traditions behind the Fourth Gos-
    pel[3]   107-124
E. RUCKSTUHL (Luzern), Johannine Language and Style. The
    Question of Their Unity[4]   125-147
J.L. MARTYN (New York), Glimpses into the History of the
    Johannine Community[5]   149-175
I. DE LA POTTERIE (Rome), Parole et esprit dans S. Jean . .   177-201

II

M. SABBE (Leuven), The Arrest of Jesus in Jn 18,1-11 and Its
    Relation to the Synoptic Gospels[6]   203-234
M.-É. BOISMARD (Jerusalem), Un procédé rédactionnel dans
    le quatrième évangile: la *Wiederaufnahme*   235-241
P. BORGEN (Trondheim), Some Jewish Exegetical Traditions
    as Background for Son of Man Sayings in John's Gospel
    (Jn 3,13-14 and context)[7]   243-258
H. THYEN (Heidelberg), Entwicklungen innerhalb der jo-
    hanneischen Theologie und Kirche im Spiegel von Joh
    21 und der Lieblingsjüngertexte des Evangeliums . . .   259-299

III

P. BONNARD (Lausanne), La première épître de Jean est-elle
    johannique?[8]   301-305
R.E. BROWN (New York), The «Mother of Jesus» in the
    Fourth Gospel   307-310
J. COPPENS (Leuven), Les logia johanniques du Fils de
    l'homme   311-315

J. DELOBEL (Leuven), The Bodmer Papyri of John. A Short
    Survey of the Methodological Problems 317-323
K.P. DONFRIED (Northampton, Mass.), Ecclesiastical Author-
    ity in 2-3 John 325-333
K. HANHART (Brussel), «About the tenth hour» ... on Nisan
    15 (Jn 1,35-40) 335-346
C.J.A. HICKLING (London), Attitudes to Judaism in the
    Fourth Gospel 347-354
Yvonne JANSSENS (Louvain), Une source gnostique du Pro-
    logue? 355-358
J. PAINTER (Cape Town), Christ and the Church in John
    1,45-51 359-362
T.E. POLLARD (Dunedin), The Father-Son and God-Believer
    Relationships according to St John: a Brief Study of
    John's Use of Prepositions 363-369
Sandra M. SCHNEIDERS (Berkeley, Calif.), History and Sym-
    bolism in the Fourth Gospel [9] 371-376
B. SCHWANK (Beuron), Efraim in Joh 11,54 [10] 377-383
J. SEYNAEVE (Kinshasa), Les verbes ἀποστέλλω et πέμπω
    dans le vocabulaire théologique de saint Jean 385-389

1. *Das Johannesevangelium*. IV. Teil: *Ergänzende Auslegungen und Exkurse* (Herders theologischer Kommentar zum Neuen Testament, 4/4), Freiburg-Basel-Wien, 1984, 9-32.

2. *Evangelica* (BETL, 60), 365-398.

3. *Essays on John* (SNTA, 17), Leuven, 1992, 87-104.

4. *Sprache und Stil im johanneischen Schrifttum. Die Frage ihrer Einheit und Einheitlichkeit*, in ID., *Die literarische Einheit des Johannesevangeliums. Der gegenwärtige Stand der einschlägigen Forschungen* (Novum Testamentum et Orbis Antiquus, 5), Freiburg (Schweiz)-Göttingen, 1987, 304-331.

5. *The Gospel of John in Christian History. Essays for Interpreters*, New York, 1978, 90-121.

6. *Studia Neotestamentica* (BETL, 98), 355-386.

7. *The Son of Man Saying in John 3,13-14*, in ID., *Logos Was the True Light and Other Essays on the Gospel of John* («Relieff». Publications Edited by the Department of Religious Studies, University of Trondheim, 9), Trondheim, 1983, 133-148.

8. *Anamnesis*, 1980, 195-200.

9. *Geschichte und Symbolik im Johannesevangelium*, in *Erbe und Auftrag* 52 (1976) 30-35.

10. *Erbe und Auftrag* 51 (1975) 346-351.

M. Delcor (éd.), *Qumrân. Sa piété, sa théologie et son milieu.* (BETL, 46), Gembloux-Leuven, 1978, 427 p.

M. Delcor (Toulouse), Avant-propos 7-8

M. Delcor, Où en sont les études qumrâniennes? . . . 11-46
H. Stegemann (Marburg), Die Qumranforschungsstelle
Marburg und ihre Aufgabenstellung. Ein Bericht . . . 47-54
E.M. Laperrousaz (Paris), La datation d'objets provenant
de Qumrân, en particulier par la méthode utilisant les
propriétés du carbone 14 55-60
E. Szyszman (Paris), Une source auxiliaire importante pour
les études qumrâniennes: les collections Firkowicz . . 61-73

I

M. Baillet (Bordeaux), Le volume VII de «Discoveries in
the Judaean Desert». Présentation 75-89
J.T. Milik (Paris), Écrits préesséniens de Qumrân: d'Hénoch
à Amram 91-106
J. van der Ploeg (Nijmegen), Une *halakha* inédite de Qumrân 107-113
Y. Yadin (Jerusalem), Le Rouleau du Temple 115-119
A.S. van der Woude (Groningen), Bemerkungen zum Gebet
des Nabonides (4Q or Nab) 121-129
B. Jongeling (Groningen), Détermination et indétermina-
tion dans 11QtgJob 131-136
H. Pabst (Marburg), Eine Sammlung von Klagen in den
Qumranfunden (4Q 179) 137-149
H. Lichtenberger (Marburg), Eine weisheitliche Mahnrede
in den Qumranfunden (4Q 185) 151-162

II

P.W. Skehan (Washington, D.C.), Qumran and Old Testa-
ment Criticism 163-182
H.W. Brownlee (Claremont), The Background of Biblical
Interpretation at Qumrân 183-193
H. Stegemann (Marburg), Religionsgeschichtliche Erwägun-
gen zu den Gottesbezeichnungen in den Qumrantexten . 195-217
J. Carmignac (Paris), La future intervention de Dieu selon
la pensée de Qumrân 219-229

A. Caquot (Paris), Le messianisme qumrânien 231-247

J. Starcky (Paris), Les Maîtres de Justice et la chronologie
de Qumrân 249-256

N. Ilg (Marburg), Überlegungen zum Verständnis von Berît
in den Qumrantexten 257-263

Sh. Talmon (Jerusalem), The Emergence of Institutionalized
Prayer in Israel in the Light of the Qumran Literature . 265-284

H.J. Fabry (Bonn), Die Wurzel Šwb in der Qumranliteratur 285-293

J. Coppens (Leuven), Le célibat essénien 295-303

A. Jaubert (Paris), Fiches de Calendrier 305-311

III

P.-M. Bogaert (Maredsous et Louvain-la-Neuve), Les *Anti-
quités bibliques* du Pseudo-Philon à la lumière des décou-
vertes de Qumrân. Observations sur l'hymnologie et
particulièrement sur le chapitre 60 313-331

M. Hengel (Tübingen), Qumrân und der Hellenismus . . 333-372

J. Coppens, Où en est le problème des analogies qumrâniennes avec le Nouveau Testament? 373-383

J. Schmitt (Strasbourg), Qumrân et la première génération
judéo-chrétienne 385-402

S. Sabugal (Roma), La mención neotestamentaria de
Damasco 403-413

M. Delcor, Conclusions. Lignes de force du Congrès . . 415-418

28 1977

J. KREMER (éd.), *Les Actes des Apôtres. Traditions, rédaction, théologie.* (BETL, 48), Gembloux-Leuven, 1979, 590 p.

J. KREMER (Wien), Einführung in die Problematik heutiger Acta-Forschung anhand von Apg 17,10-13 11-20

I

C.M. MARTINI (Roma), La tradition textuelle des Actes des Apôtres et les tendances de l'Église ancienne[1] 21-35

W.C. VAN UNNIK (Utrecht), Luke's Second Book and the Rules of Hellenistic Historiography 37-60

M. RESE (Münster), Die Funktion der alttestamentlichen Zitate und Anspielungen in den Reden der Apostelgeschichte 61-79

G.D. KILPATRICK (Oxford), Some Quotations in Acts[2] . . 81-97

E. GRÄSSER (Bochum), Die Parusieerwartung in der Apostelgeschichte 99-127

F. HAHN (München), Das Problem alter christologischer Überlieferungen in der Apostelgeschichte unter besonderer Berüksichtigung von Act 3,19-21 129-154

J. SCHMITT (Strasbourg), Kérygme pascal et lecture scripturaire dans l'instruction d'Antioche (Act. 13,23-37) . . 155-167

F. NEIRYNCK (Leuven), The Miracle Stories in the Acts of the Apostles. An Introduction[3] 169-213

G. SCHNEIDER (Bochum), Stephanus, die Hellenisten und Samaria 215-240

M. SABBE (Leuven), The Son of Man Saying in Acts 7,56[4] . 241-279

C.K. BARRETT (Durham), Light on the Holy Spirit from Simon Magus (Acts 8,4-25) 281-295

J. JERVELL (Oslo), Paul in the Acts of the Apostles. Tradition, History, Theology 297-306

J. LAMBRECHT (Leuven), Paul's Farewell-Address at Miletus (Acts 20,17-38) 307-337

F. BOVON (Genève), Le Saint-Esprit, l'Église et les relations humaines selon Actes 20,36–21,16[5] 339-358

J. DUPONT (Ottignies), La conclusion des Actes et son rapport à l'ensemble de l'ouvrage de Luc[6] 359-404

J. COPPENS (Leuven), L'imposition des mains dans les Actes des Apôtres 405-438

II

E. BAMMEL (Oxford), Der Text von Apostelgeschichte 15 . 439-446

M. WILCOX (Bangor), Luke and the Bezan Text of Acts . . 447-455

E. PLÜMACHER (Berlin), Die Apostelgeschichte als historische
Monographie 457-466

M. DUMAIS (Ottawa), Le langage des discours d'évangélisa-
tion des Actes: une forme de langage symbolique? . . 467-474

S.J. NOORDA (Amsterdam), Scene and Summary. A Proposal
for Reading Acts 4,32–5,16 475-483

R. McL. WILSON (St. Andrews), Simon and Gnostic Origins 485-491

E. NELLESSEN (Bonn), Die Presbyter der Gemeinden in
Lykaonien und Pisidien (Apg 14,23) 493-498

C.J.A. HICKLING (London), The Portrait of Paul in Acts 26 499-503

R.H. FULLER (Alexandria, Va), Was Paul Baptized? . . . 505-508

W. KIRCHSCHLÄGER (Wien), Fieberheilung in Apg 28 und Lk 4 509-521

P.G. MÜLLER (Kerkrade/Rolduc), Die jüdische Entscheidung
gegen Jesus nach der Apostelgeschichte 523-531

J. PATHRAPANKAL (Bangalore), Christianity as a «Way»
according to the Acts of the Apostles 533-539

B. DEHANDSCHUTTER (Leiden), La persécution des chrétiens
dans les Actes des Apôtres 541-546

1. *La parola di Dio* (1980), 165–179.
2. *The Principles and Practice of New Testament Textual Criticism: Collected Essays.*
Edited by J.K. ELLIOTT (BETL, 96), Leuven, 1990, 380-399.
3. *Evangelica* (BETL, 60), 835-879.
4. *Studia Neotestamentica* (BETL, 98), 137-175.
5. *L'œuvre de Luc. Études d'exégèse et de théologie* (Lectio Divina, 130), Paris, 1987,
121-194; G.T. *Der Heilige Geist, die Kirche und die menschlichen Beziehungen nach
Apostelgeschichte 20,26-21,16*, in *Lukas in neuer Sicht. Gesammelte Aufsätze* (Biblisch-
theologische Studien, 8), Neukirchen-Vluyn, 1985, 181-204.
6. *Nouvelles Études sur les Actes des Apôtres*, 1984, 457-511.

M. Gilbert (éd.), *La Sagesse dans l'Ancien Testament.*
(BETL, 51), Gembloux-Leuven, 1979; Leuven, [2]1989, 455 p.

M. Gilbert (Louvain-Roma), Avant-propos 7-13

I

L'AMPLEUR DU COURANT DE SAGESSE

H. Cazelles (Paris), Les nouvelles études sur Sumer (Alster)
et Mari (Marzal) nous aident-elles à situer les origines de
la sagesse israélite? 17-27
C. Brekelmans (Leuven), Wisdom Influence in Deutero-
nomy 28-38
J. Vermeylen (Bruxelles), Le Proto-Isaïe et la sagesse d'Israël 39-58
J. Luyten (Leuven), Psalm 73 and Wisdom 59-81
J.P.M. van der Ploeg (Nijmegen), Le Psaume 119 et la
sagesse 82-84
N.J. Tromp (Utrecht), Wisdom and the Canticle. Ct., 8,6c-
7b: text, character, message and import 88-95
J.L. Crenshaw (Nashville), Questions, dictons et épreuves
impossibles 96-111
S. Amsler (Lausanne), La sagesse de la femme 112-116
P.-É. Bonnard (Lyon), De la sagesse personnifiée dans
l'Ancien Testament à la Sagesse en personne dans le
Nouveau 117-149

II

LES LIVRES SAPIENTIAUX DE L'ANCIEN TESTAMENT

R.N. Whybray (Hull), Yahweh-sayings and their Contexts
in Proverbs, 10,1–22,16 153-165
W. McKane (St. Andrews), Functions of Language and
Objectives of Discourse according to Proverbs, 10–30 . 166-185
B. Lang (Tübingen), Schule und Unterricht im alten Israel . 186-201
M. Gilbert, Le discours de la Sagesse en Proverbes, 8.
Structure et cohérence 202-218
G. Fohrer (Jerusalem), Dialog und Kommunikation im
Buche Hiob 219-230
J. Lévêque (Paris), Anamnèse et disculpation: la conscience
du juste en Job, 29–31 231-248

D. Lys (Montpellier), L'Être et le Temps. Communication de
    Qohèlèth   249-258
N. Lohfink (Frankfurt a.M.), War Kohelet ein Frauenfeind?
    Ein Versuch, die Logik und den Gegenstand von Koh.,
    7,23–8,1a herauszufinden   259-287
J. Coppens (Leuven), La structure de l'Ecclésiaste   288-292
J. Marböck (Graz), Sir., 38,24–39,11: Der Schriftgelehrte
    Weise. Ein Beitrag zu Gestalt und Werk Ben Siras . .   293-316
G.L. Prato (Roma), La lumière interprète de la sagesse dans
    la tradition textuelle de Ben Sira   317-346
P. Beauchamp (Paris), Épouser la Sagesse – ou n'épouser
    qu'elle? Une énigme du Livre de la Sagesse   347-369
F. Raurell (Barcelona), The Religious Meaning of «Doxa»
    in the Book of Wisdom   370-383
J.M. Reese (New York), Can Paul Ricœur's Method Contri-
    bute to Interpreting the Book of Wisdom?   384-396

Notes additionnelles – Additional Notes – Nachträge
    (1989)   397-425

M. Gilbert, Une décennie sur les livres sapientiaux: 1979-1989 (399-406).
J. Vermeylen (407-408). L. Luyten (409-410). J. L. Crenshaw (410).
    S. Amsler (411). R. N. Whybray (411-412). B. Lang (412-414).
    M. Gilbert (414-415). J. Lévêque (416-417). N. Lohfink (417-420).
    J. Marböck (421-423). G.L Prato (423). F. Raurell (424).
    J.M. Reese (424-425).

J. LAMBRECHT (éd.), *L'Apocalypse johannique et l'Apocalyptique dans le Nouveau Testament.*
(BETL, 53), Gembloux-Leuven, 1980, 458 p.

J. LAMBRECHT (Leuven), The Book of Revelation and Apocalyptic in the New Testament   11-18

I

L'APOCALYPSE

U. VANNI (Roma), L'Apocalypse johannique. État de la question   21-46

P.-M. BOGAERT (Louvain-la-Neuve), Les apocalypses contemporaines de Baruch, d'Esdras et de Jean . . .   47-68

Y. JANSSENS (Louvain-la-Neuve), Apocalypses de Nag Hammadi   69-75

J. LAMBRECHT, A Structuration of Revelation 4,1–22,5 . .   77-104

E. SCHÜSSLER FIORENZA (Notre Dame), Apokalypsis and Propheteia. The Book of Revelation in the Context of Early Christian Prophecy   105-128

L. HARTMAN (Uppsala), Form and Message. A Preliminary Discussion of «Partial Texts» in Rev 1–3 and 22,6ff. .   129-149

J. DELOBEL (Leuven), Le texte de l'Apocalypse: Problèmes de méthode   151-166

G. MUSSIES (Utrecht), The Greek of the Book of Revelation   167-177

J. LUST (Leuven), The Order of the Final Events in Revelation and in Ezekiel   179-183

A. YARBRO COLLINS (Chicago), Revelation 18: Taunt-Song or Dirge?[1]   185-204

M. WILCOX (Bangor), Tradition and Redaction of Rev 21,9–22,5   205-215

A.P. VAN SCHAIK (Nijmegen), Ἄλλος ἄγγελος in Apk 14 .   217-228

J. COPPENS (Leuven), La mention d'un Fils d'homme angélique en Ap 14,14   229

P. PRIGENT (Strasbourg), Le temps et le Royaume dans l'Apocalypse   231-245

T. HOLTZ (Halle-Saale), Gott in der Apokalypse   247-265

M. DE JONGE (Leiden), The Use of the Expression ὁ χριστός in the Apocalypse of John[2]   267-281

B. Dehandschutter (Leiden), The Meaning of Witness in
the Apocalypse   283-288
O. Böcher (Mainz), Das Verhältnis der Apokalypse des
Johannes zum Evangelium des Johannes   289-301

II

Le Nouveau Testament

A.S. Geyser (Johannesburg), Some Salient New Testament
Passages on the Restoration of the Twelve Tribes of
Israel   305-310
M. Rese (Münster), Die Rolle Israels im apokalyptischen
Denken des Paulus   311-318
G. Mayeda (Tokyo), Apocalyptic in the Epistle to the
Romans – An Outline   319-323
R.F. Collins (Leuven), Tradition, Redaction, and Exhortation
in 1 Th 4,13–5,11   325-343
J. Coppens, Le katechon et le katechôn: derniers obstacles à
la parousie du Seigneur Jésus   345-348
T. Korteweg (Leiden), «You will seek me and you will not
find me» (Jn 7,34). An Apocalyptic Pattern in Johannine
Theology   349-354
R. Pesch (Freiburg), Markus 13   355-368
F. Neirynck (Leuven), Marc 13. Examen critique de l'inter-
prétation de R. Pesch [3]   369-401
E. Lövestam (Lund), The ἡ γενεὰ αὕτη Eschatology in Mk
13,30 parr.   403-413
G.R. Beasley-Murray (Louisville), Jesus and Apocalyptic:
With Special Reference to Mark 14,62   415-429

1. Cf. *Crisis and Catharsis. The Power of the Apocalypse*, Philadelphia, 1984.

2. *Jewish Eschatology, Early Christian Christology and the Testaments of the Twelve Patriarchs: Collected Essays* (SupplNT, 63), Leiden, 1991, 87-101.

3. *Evangelica* (BETL, 60), 565-597.

31 1980

P.-M. Bogaert (éd.), *Le Livre de Jérémie. Le prophète et son milieu. Les oracles et leur transmission.*
(BETL, 54), Leuven, 1981, 410 p.; ²1997, 448 p.

P.-M. Bogaert (Louvain-la-Neuve), Introduction   13-18

I

LE CADRE HISTORIQUE

H. Cazelles (Paris), La vie de Jérémie dans son contexte national et international   21-39

J. Scharbert (München), Jeremia und die Reform des Joschija   40-57

W.L. Holladay (Newton Centre), A Coherent Chronology of Jeremiah's Early Career   58-73

G. Brunet (Paris), Jérémie et les Qînôt de son adversaire .   74-79

II

L'ENVIRONNEMENT LITTÉRAIRE

H. Weippert (IJsselstein), Der Beitrag ausserbiblischer Prophetentexte zum Verständnis der Prosareden des Jeremiabuches   83-104

M. Gilbert (Roma), Jérémie en conflit avec les sages? . .   105-118

J. Lust (Leuven), «Gathering and Return» in Jeremiah and Ezekiel   119-142

III

LA SEPTANTE DE JÉRÉMIE AU SERVICE DE LA CRITIQUE LITTÉRAIRE

E. Tov (Jerusalem), Some Aspects of the Textual and Literary History of the Book of Jeremiah   145-167

P.-M. Bogaert, De Baruch à Jérémie. Les deux rédactions conservées du livre de Jérémie   168-173

IV
Exégèse du Livre de Jérémie

B. Renaud (Strasbourg), Jér 1: Structure et théologie de la
rédaction   177-196
S. Herrmann (Bochum), Jeremia – der Prophet und die Ver-
fasser des Buches Jeremia   197-214
J.A. Soggin (Roma), The Ark of the Covenant, Jeremiah
3,16   215-221
P.-M. Bogaert, Les mécanismes rédactionnels en Jér 10,1-16
(LXX et TM) et la signification des suppléments . . .   222-238
J. Vermeylen (Bruxelles), Essai de Redaktiongeschichte des
«Confessions de Jérémie»   239-270
F.D. Hubmann (Graz), Jer 18,18-23 im Zusammenhang der
Konfessionen   271-296
W.A.M. Beuken (Amsterdam) & H.W.M van Grol (Jerusa-
lem), Jeremiah 14,1–15,9: A Situation of Distress and its
Hermeneutics. Unity and Diversity of Form – Drama-
tic Development   297-342
C. Brekelmans (Leuven), Jeremiah 18,1-12 and its Redac-   343-350
tion . . . .
N. Lohfink (München), Der junge Jeremia als Propagandist
und Poet. Zum Grundstock von Jer 30–31   351-368
C. de Jong (De Lier), Deux oracles contre les Nations, reflets
de la politique étrangère de Joaqim   369-379

Appendice

P.-M. Bogaert, Le livre de Jérémie 1981-1996   411-417

Notes additionnelles – Additional Notes – Nachträge . . .   397-425

H. Cazelles (418-422); J. Scharbert (422-424); W.L. Holladay (425-426);
H. Weippert (426-427); M. Gilbert (427-428); J. Lust (428-430); E. Tov (430);
P. M. Bogaert (430-432); S. Herrmann (433); P.-M. Bogaert (433-434); J. Vermeylen
(435-436); F.D. Hubmann (436-439); N. Lohfink (439-445)

32 1981

J. Delobel (éd.), *Logia. Les paroles de Jésus. – The Sayings of Jesus. Mémorial Joseph Coppens.*
(BETL, 59), Leuven, 1982, 647 p.

F. Neirynck (Leuven), J. Coppens, fondateur des Journées Bibliques de Louvain[1]   9-19

J. Delobel (Leuven), Introduction   23-27
F. Neirynck, Recent Developments in the Study of Q[2] . .   29-75
A. Vögtle (Freiburg), Bezeugt die Logienquelle die authentische Redeweise Jesu vom «Menschensohn»?[3] . . .   77-99
C.E. Carlston (Newton Centre), Wisdom and Eschatology in Q   101-119
H. Schürmann (Erfurt), Das Zeugnis der Redenquelle für die Basileia-Verkündigung Jesu[4]   121-200
J. Dupont (Ottignies), La transmission des paroles de Jésus sur la lampe et la mesure dans Marc 4,21-25 et dans la tradition Q[5]   201-236
S. Légasse (Toulouse), L'oracle contre «cette génération» (Mt 23,34-36 par. Lc 11,49-51) et la polémique judéochrétienne dans la source des Logia   237-256
R.A. Edwards (Milwaukee), Matthew's Use of Q in Chapter Eleven   257-275
J. Lambrecht (Leuven), Q-Influence on Mark 8,34–9,1 . .   277-304
A. Denaux (Brugge), Der Spruch von den zwei Wegen im Rahmen des Epilogs der Bergpredigt (Mt 7,13-14 par. Lk 13,23-24). Tradition und Redaktion   305-335
J.M. Van Cangh (Louvain-la-Neuve), «Par l'esprit de Dieu – par le doigt de Dieu» Mt 12,28 par. Lc 11,20 . . .   337-342
C.M. Tuckett (Manchester), Luke 4,16-30, Isaiah and Q .   343-354
V. Fusco (Napoli), L'accord mineur Mt 13,11a par. Lc 8.10a contre Mc 4,11a   355-361
M. Sabbe (Leuven), Can Mt 11,27 and par. Lk 10,22 Be Called a Johannine Logion?[6]   363-371
H.-T. Wrege (Kassel), Zur Rolle des Geistwortes in frühchristlichen Traditionen (Lc 12,1 parr.)   373-377
P. Vassiliadis (Thessaloniki), The Original Order of Q. Some Residual Cases   379-387

J.M. ROBINSON (Claremont), Early Collections of Jesus' Sayings 389-394

D. ZELLER (Luzern), Redaktionsprozesse und wechselnder «Sitz im Leben» beim Q-Material 395-409

R. PIPER (St Andrews), Matthew 7,7-11 par. Lk 11,9-13: Evidence of Design and Argument in the Collection of Jesus' Sayings 411-418

A.D. JACOBSON (Moorhead, Minn.), The Literary Unity of Q. Lc 10,2-16 and Parallels as a Test Case 419-423

C.J.A. HICKLING (London), The Plurality of «Q» 425-429

J. DELOBEL, The Sayings of Jesus in the Textual Tradition. Variant Readings in the Greek Manuscripts of the Gospels 431-457

S.J. NOORDA (Amsterdam), «Cure yourself, doctor!» (Luke 4,23). Classical Parallels to an Alleged Saying of Jesus . 459-467

M. WILCOX (Bangor), Ταλιθα κουμ(ι) in Mk 5,41 469-476

H. RÄISÄNEN (Helsinki), Zur Herkunft von Markus 7,15[7] . 477-484

J.-M. MAGNE (Paris), Les paroles sur la coupe 485-490

W.S. VORSTER (Pretoria), Redaction, Contextualisation and the Sayings of Jesus 491-500

G.W. BUCHANAN (Washington), Chreias in the New Testament 501-505

B. DEHANDSCHUTTER (Leiden), L'Évangile de Thomas comme collection de paroles de Jésus 507-515

J.-M. SEVRIN (Louvain-la-Neuve), Paroles et paraboles de Jésus dans des écrits gnostiques coptes 517-528

T. BAARDA (Amsterdam), 2 Clem 12 and the Sayings of Jesus [8] 529-556

F. NEIRYNCK & F. VAN SEGBROECK (Leuven), Q Bibliography 557-582

1. *ETL* 57 (1981) 274-292.

2. *Evangelica II* (BETL, 99), Leuven, 1991, 409-455.

3. *Offenbarungsgeschehen und Wirkungsgeschichte. Neutestamentliche Beiträge*, Freiburg, 1985, 50-69.

4. *Gottes Reich - Jesu Geschick. Jesu ureigener Tod im Licht seiner Basileia-Verkündigung*, Freiburg, 1983, 65-152.

5. *Études sur les Évangiles Synoptiques*, 1985, 259-294.

6. *Studia Neotestamentica* (BETL, 98), 399-407.

7. *The Torah and Christ* (PFES, 45), Helsinki, 1986, 209-218.

8. *Early Transmission of Words of Jesus. Thomas, Tatian and the Text of the New Testament. A Collection of Studies*, ed. J. HELDERMAN & S.J. NOORDA, Amsterdam, 1983, 261-288.

33 1983   viii. 17-19

N. LOHFINK (ed.), *Das Deuteronomium. Entstehung, Gestalt und Botschaft / Deuteronomy: Origin, Form and Message.*
(BETL, 68), Leuven, 1985, XI-382 p.

N. LOHFINK (Frankfurt am Main), Einführung   1-5

I
FORSCHUNGSGESCHICHTE

M.J. PAUL (Leiden), Hilkiah and the Law (2 Kings 22) in the
17th and 18th Centuries: Some Influences on W.M.L. de
Wette   9-12
J. LUST (Leuven), A. Van Hoonacker and Deuteronomy   .   13-23
N. LOHFINK, Zur neueren Diskussion über 2 Kön 22–23. .   24-48

II
DAS DEUTERONOMISCHE PHÄNOMEN
UND DAS BUCH ALS GANZES

S. AMSLER (Lausanne), Loi orale et loi écrite dans le Deuté-   51-54
ronome . . . .
J. HALBE (Preetz), «Gemeinschaft, die Welt unterbricht»:
Grundfragen und -inhalte deuteronomischer Theologie
und Überlieferungsbildung im Lichte der Ursprungs-
bedingungen alttestamentlichen Rechts   55-75
M. WEINFELD (Jerusalem), The Emergence of the Deuterono-
mic Movement: The Historical Antecedents   76-98
H. CAZELLES (Paris), Droit public dans le Deutéronome . .   99-106
L.J. HOPPE (Chicago), Jerusalem in the Deuteronomistic
History   107-110
C.J. LABUSCHAGNE (Groningen), Divine Speech in Deuter-
onomy   111-126

III
TEXTE UND EINZELPROBLEME IM DEUTERONOMIUM

L. LABERGE (Ottawa), La Septante de Dt 1–11: Pour une
étude du «texte»   129-134
D.L. CHRISTENSEN (Berkeley), Form and Structure in Deuteronomy 1–11   135-144
J. VAN GOUDOEVER (Amsterdam), The Liturgical Significance
of the Date in Dt 1,3   145-148

L. PERLITT (Göttingen), Deuteronomium 1–3 im Streit der exegetischen Methoden 149-163

C. BREKELMANS (Leuven), Deuteronomy 5: Its Place and Function 164-173

J. VERMEYLEN (Bruxelles), Les sections narratives de Deut 5–11 et leur relation à Ex 19–34 174-207

C.T. BEGG (Washington, D.C.), The Destruction of the Calf (Exod 32,20/Deut 9,21) 208-251

G. BRAULIK (Wien), Die Abfolge der Gesetze in Deuteronomium 12–26 und der Dekalog 252-272

S.A. KAUFMAN (Cincinnati), Deuteronomy 15 and Recent Research on the Dating of P 273-276

F. GARCÍA LÓPEZ (Salamanca), Le roi d'Israël: Dt 17,14-20   277-297

C. LOCHER (Zürich), Deuteronomium 22,13-21: Vom Prozeß-protokoll zum kasuistischen Gesetz 298-303

M. ANBAR (Tel-Aviv), The Story about the Building of an Altar on Mount Ebal: The History of Its Composition and the Question of the Centralization of the Cult . . 304-309

A. ROFÉ (Jerusalem), The Covenant in the Land of Moab (Dt 28,69–30,20): Historico-literary, Comparative, and Formcritical Considerations 310-320

A.D.H. MAYES (Dublin), Deuteronomy 29, Joshua 9, and the Place of the Gibeonites in Israel 321-325

W.L. HOLLADAY (Newton Centre), A Proposal for Reflections in the Book of Jeremiah of the Seven-Year Recitation of the Law in Deuteronomy (Deut 31,10-13) . . 326-328

P.-M. BOGAERT (Louvain-la-Neuve), Les trois rédactions conservées et la forme originale de l'envoi du Cantique de Moïse (Dt 32,43) 329-340

J. LUYTEN (Leuven), Primeval and Eschatological Overtones in the Song of Moses (Dt 32,1-43) 341-347

IV

DEUTERONOMISTISCHES GESCHICHTSWERK

H.-J. FABRY (Bonn) Spuren des Pentateuchredaktors in Jos 4,21 ff.: Anmerkungen zur Deuteronomismus-Rezeption   351-356

G. VANONI (Wien-Mödling), Beobachtungen zur deuteronomistischen Terminologie in 2 Kön 23,25–25,30 . . 357-362

Appendix: A. Van Hoonacker Bibliography 363-368

34 1984 viii. 27-29

A. VANHOYE, *L'apôtre Paul. Personnalité, style et conception du ministère.*
(BETL, 73), Leuven, 1986, XIII-470 p.

A. VANHOYE, Introduction . . . . IX-XIII

I
PERSONNALITÉ ET STYLE

A. VANHOYE (Roma), Personnalité de Paul et exégèse pauli-
nienne 3-15
H.D. BETZ (Chicago), The Problem of Rhetoric and Theo-
logy according to the Apostle Paul 16-48
W. WUELLNER (Berkeley), Paul as Pastor. The Function of
Rhetorical Questions in First Corinthians 49-77
B. STANDAERT (Brugge), La rhétorique ancienne dans saint
Paul 78-92
J.H. ROBERTS (Pretoria), Pauline Transitions to the Letter 93-99
Body . . . .

II
CONCEPTION DU MINISTÈRE

W. SCHRAGE (Bonn), Das Apostolische Amt des Paulus nach
1 Kor 4,14-17 103-119
J. LAMBRECHT (Leuven), The nekrōsis of Jesus. Ministry and
Suffering in 2 Cor 4,7-15 120-143
W. RADL (Augsburg), Alle Mühe umsonst? Paulus und der
Gottesknecht 144-149
G. DAUTZENBERG (Giessen), Motive der Selbstdarstellung des
Paulus in 2 Kor 2,14–7,4 150-162
M. CARREZ (Paris), Réalité christologique et référence apos-
tolique de l'apôtre Paul en présence d'une église divisée
(2 Cor 10–13) 163-183
K. KERTELGE (Münster), Der Ort des Amtes in der Ekklesio-
logie des Paulus 184-202
N. BAUMERT (Frankfurt), Charisma und Amt bei Paulus . 203-228
J.-N. ALETTI (Roma), L'autorité apostolique de Paul.
Théorie et pratique 229-246
P. VASSILIADIS (Thessaloniki), ΣΤΑΥΡΟΣ: Centre of the Pauline
Soteriology and Apostolic Ministry 247-253

J. PONTHOT (Louvain-la-Neuve), L'expression cultuelle du
    ministère paulinien selon Rom 15,16   254-262

III
PROBLÈMES PARTICULIERS

F. NEIRYNCK (Leuven), Paul and the Sayings of Jesus [1] . .   265-321
A. MEN (Semkhoz), The Messianic Eschatology of St Paul in
    connexion with the Primitive Preaching of the Gospel .   322-323
C.J. ROETZEL (St Paul, Minnesota), Theodidaktoi and Hand-
    work in Philo and I Thessalonians   324-331
W. KIRCHSCHLÄGER (Luzern), Zu Herkunft und Aussage von
    Gal 1,4   332-339
G. BERÉNYI (Roma), Gal 2,20: A Pre-Pauline or a Pauline
    Text?[2]   340-344
C.M. TUCKETT (Manchester), Deuteronomy 21,33 and Paul's
    Conversion   345-350
N. WALTER (Naumburg), Paulus und die Gegner des Christus-
    evangeliums in Galatien   351-356
J.C. O'NEILL (Cambridge), 1 Corinthians 7,14 and Infant
    Baptism   357-361
A.J.M. WEDDERBURN (St Andrews), Paul's Use of the Phrase
    'in Christ' and 'with Christ'[3]   362
C.K. BARRETT (Durham), Boasting (καυχᾶσθαι, κτλ.) in the
    Pauline Epistles   363-368
J. DELOBEL (Leuven), 1 Cor 11,2-16: Towards a Coherent
    Interpretation   369-389
R. PENNA (Roma), L'évolution de l'attitude de Paul envers
    les Juifs   390-421
M. RESE (Münster), Die Rettung der Juden nach Römer 11   422-430

1. *Evangelica II* (BETL, 99), 511-567.
    2. Compare *Biblica* 65 (1984) 490-537.
    3. Short version of the article *Some Observations on Paul's Use of the Phrases 'in Christ' and 'with Christ'*, in *JSNT* 25 (1985) 83-97.

35 1985   viii. 27-29

J. Lust (ed.), *Ezekiel and his Book. Textual and Literary Criticism and their Interrelation.*
(BETL, 74), Leuven, 1986, x-387 p.

J. Lust, Introduction: Ezekiel and his Book   1-3

I

Textual Criticism
and Its Relation with Literary Criticism

J. Lust (Leuven), The Use of Textual Witnesses for the
Establishment of the Text. The Shorter and Longer
Texts of Ezekiel   7-20
P.-M. Bogaert (Louvain-la-Neuve), Les deux rédactions
conservées (LXX et TM) d'Ézéchiel 7   21-47
J. Lust, The Final Text and Textual Criticism. Ez 39,28 .   48-54
M. Dijkstra (Cairo), The Glosses in Ezekiel Reconsidered:
Aspects of Textual Transmission in Ezekiel 10 . . .   55-77
V. Spottorno (Madrid), Some Lexical Aspects in the Greek
Text of Ezekiel   78-84
F. Raurell (Barcelona), The Polemical Role of the
ΑΡΧΟΝΤΕΣ and ΑΦΗΓΟΥΜΕΝΟΙ in Ez LXX . .   85-89
J. Lust, Ezekiel Manuscripts in Qumran. Preliminary
Edition of 4Q Ez a and b   90-100
M.J. Mulder (Leiden), Die neue Pešitta-Ausgabe von Eze-   101-110
chiel . . . .
C.M.L. Verdegaal, The Jewish Influence on the Ezekiel-
Translation of the English and Dutch Authorized Ver-
sions   111-119

II

Literary Criticism, Its Methods
and Its Relation to Other Approaches

M. Greenberg (Jerusalem), What Are Valid Criteria for
Determining Inauthentic Matter in Ezekiel?   123-135
J. Becker (Simpelveld), Ez 8–11 als einheitliche Komposition
in einem pseudepigraphischen Ezechielbuch   136-150
F.L. Hossfeld (Bonn), Die Tempelvision Ez 8–11 im Licht
unterschiedlicher methodischer Zugänge   151-165
D. Baltzer (Essen), Literarkritische und literarhistorische
Anmerkungen zur Heilsprophetie im Ezechiel-Buch . .   166-181

L. BOADT (Washington), Rhetorical Strategies in Ezekiel's Oracles of Judgment 182-200

N. TROMP (Utrecht), The Paradox of Ezekiel's Prophetic Mission. Towards a Semiotic Approach of Ezekiel 3,22-27 201-213

J. PONS (Montpellier), Le vocabulaire d'Éz 20. Le prophète s'oppose à la vision deutéronomiste de l'histoire . . . 214-233

H. SIMIAN-YOFRE (Rome), La métaphore d'Ézéchiel 15 . . 234-247

B. WILLMES (Duisburg), Differenzierende Prophezeiungen in Ez 34 248-254

M. NOBILE (Roma), Beziehung zwischen Ez 32,17-32 und der Gog-Perikope (Ez 38–39) im Lichte der Endredaktion . 255-259

R. RENDTORFF (Heidelberg), Ez 20 und 36,16ff im Rahmen der Komposition des Buches Ezechiel[1] 260-265

H.F. FUHS (Würzburg), Ez 24. Überlegungen zu Tradition und Redaktion des Ezechielbuches 266-282

R.E. CLEMENTS (Cambridge), The Chronology of Redaction in Ez 1–24 283-294

III

THE MESSAGE OF THE BOOK
AND ITS RELATION WITH OTHER BIBLICAL
AND NON-BIBLICAL LITERATURE

B. LANG (Paderborn), Street Theater, Raising the Dead, and the Zoroastrian Connection in Ezekiel's Prophecy . . 297-316

P. JOYCE (Oxford), Ezekiel and Individual Responsibility . 317-321

L. MONLOUBOU (Toulouse), La signification du culte selon Ézéchiel 322-329

C. DOHMEN (Bonn), Das Problem der Gottesbeschreibung im Ezechielbuch 330-334

B. RENAUD (Strasbourg), L'alliance éternelle d'Éz 16,59-63 et l'alliance nouvelle de Jér 31,31-34 335-339

C. BEGG (Washington), The Non-mention of Ezekiel in the Deuteronomistic History, the Book of Jeremiah and the Chronistic History 340-343

J. VAN GOUDOEVER (Amstelveen), Ezekiel Sees in Exile a New Temple-City at the Beginning of a Jobel Year 344-349

B. MAARSINGH (Amersfoort), Das Schwertlied in Ez 21,13-22 und das Erra-Gedicht 350-358

A. LEMAIRE (Vitry sur Seine), Les formules de datation dans Ézéchiel à la lumière des données épigraphiques récentes 359-366

1. *Kanon und Theologie. Vorarbeiten zu einer Theologie des Alten Testaments*, Neukirchen-Vluyn, 1991, 180-184.

36 1986 viii. 26-28

J.-M. SEVRIN (ed.), *The New Testament in Early Christianity / La réception des écrits néotestamentaires dans le christianisme primitif.* (BETL, 86), Leuven, 1989, XVI-406 p.

J.-M. SEVRIN, Introduction . . . . IX-XIV

I

B. ALAND (Münster), Die Rezeption des neutestamentlichen Textes in den ersten Jahrhunderten 1-38
A. LINDEMANN (Bielefeld), Der Apostel Paulus im 2. Jahrhundert 39-67

II

J.-M. SEVRIN (Louvain-la-Neuve), L'écriture du IV\ :sup: évangile comme phénomène de réception: L'exemple de Jn 6 . . 69-83
J. BEUTLER (Frankfurt), Krise und Untergang der johanneischen Gemeinde: Das Zeugnis der Johannesbriefe . 85-103
J. KAHMANN (Witten), The Second Letter of Peter and the Letter of Jude: Their Mutual Relationship 105-121

III

F. NEIRYNCK (Leuven), The Apocryphal Gospels and the Gospel of Mark[1]. 123-175
M.-É. BOISMARD (Jerusalem), Une tradition para-synoptique attestée par les Pères anciens 176-195
C. M. TUCKETT (Manchester), Synoptic Tradition in the Didache 197-230
P. F. BEATRICE (Padova), Une citation de l'Évangile de Matthieu dans l'Épître de Barnabé 231-245
J. VERHEYDEN (Leuven), L'Ascension d'Isaïe et l'Évangile de Matthieu. Examen de AI 3,13-18 247-274
B. DEHANDSCHUTTER (Leuven), Polycarp's Epistle to the Philippians: An Early Example of «Reception» . . . 275-291
J. DELOBEL (Leuven), The Lord's Prayer in the Textual Tradition. A Critique of Recent Theories and Their View on Marcion's Role 293-309
T. BAARDA (Utrecht), «A Staff only, not a Stick». Disharmony of the Gospels and the Harmony of Tatian (Matthew 10,9f.; Mark 6,8f.; Luke 9,3 and 10,4) 311-333

IV

1. *Evangelica II* (BETL, 99), 715-767.
2. *Novum Testamentum* 30 (1988) 158-168.

37 1987   viii. 19-21

J. VERMEYLEN (ed.), *The Book of Isaiah | Le Livre d'Isaïe. Les oracles et leurs relectures. Unité et complexité de l'ouvrage.*
(BETL, 81), Leuven, 1989, x-472 p.

J. VERMEYLEN, Avant-propos   1-4
J. LUST, Homage C. Brekelmans   5-8
Bibliography C. Brekelmans   9-10

I
LE LIVRE D'ISAÏE DANS SON ENSEMBLE

J. VERMEYLEN (Bruxelles), L'unité du livre d'Isaïe   11-53
O. KAISER (Marburg), Literarkritik und Tendenzkritik.
    Überlegungen zur Methode des Jesajaexegese   55-71
R. RENDTORFF (Heidelberg), Jesaja 6 im Rahmen der Komposition des Jesajabuches [1]   73-82
E. TALSTRA (Amsterdam), Grammar and Prophetic Texts.
    Computer-Assisted Syntactical Research in Isaiah . .   83-91
G.I. DAVIES (Cambridge), The Destiny of the Nations in the Book of Isaiah   93-120
C.T. BEGG (Washington), Babylon in the Book of Isaiah .   121-125
A. VAN DER KOOIJ (Utrecht), The Septuagint of Isaiah:
    Translation and Interpretation   127-133
J.-C. HAELEWYCK (Louvain-la-Neuve), L'édition de la *Vetus Latina* d'Isaïe   135-145
P.-M. BOGAERT (Louvain-la-Neuve), L'organisation des grands recueils prophétiques   147-153
P.C. BEENTJES (Utrecht), Relations between Ben Sira and the Book of Isaiah. Some Methodical Observations . . .   155-159
J. VAN RUITEN (Amsterdam), The Influence and Development of Is 65,17 in 1 En 91,16   161-166

II
LE PROTO-ISAÏE (IS 1-39)

C. BREKELMANS (Leuven), Deuteronomistic Influence in Isaiah 1–12   167-176
P. BOVATI (Rome), Le langage juridique du prophète Isaïe .   177-196
N.J. TROMP (Utrecht), Un démasquage graduel. Lecture immanente d'Is 5,1-7   197-202

A.L.H.M. VAN WIERINGEN (Eindhoven), Jesaja 6–12: Die Vegetationsbildsprache und die prophetische Struktur . 203-207

M. NOBILE (Roma), Jes 6 und Ez 1,1–3,15: Vergleich und Funktion im jeweiligen redaktionellen Kontext . . . 209-216

Y. GITAY (Beer Sheva), Isaiah and the Syro-Ephraimite War 217-230

J. HØGENHAVEN (Kopenhagen), Die symbolischen Namen in Jesaja 7 und 8 im Rahmen der sogenannten «Denkschrift» des Propheten 231-235

A.K. JENKINS (Cardiff), The Development of the Isaiah Tradition in Is 13–23 237-251

R.E. CLEMENTS (Cambridge), Isaiah 14,22-27: A Central Passage Reconsidered 253-262

S. AMSLER (Lausanne), Des visions de Zacharie à l'apocalypse d'Esaïe 24–27 263-273

J. LUST (Leuven), Isaiah 34 and the ḥerem 275-286

III
LE DEUTÉRO- ET LE TRITO-ISAÏE (Is 40-66)

H.-J. HERMISSON (Tübingen), Einheit und Komplexität Deuterojesajas. Probleme der Redaktionsgeschichte von Jes 40–55 287-312

J. VAN GOUDOEVER (Amstelveen), The Celebration of the Torah in the Second Isaiah 313-317

J.F.A. SAWYER (Newcastle), Christian Interpretations of Isaiah 45:8 319-323

P. BEAUCHAMP (Paris), Lecture et relectures du quatrième chant du Serviteur. D'Isaïe à Jean 325-355

H.C. SPYKERBOER (Brisbane), Isaiah 55:1-5: The Climax of Deutero-Isaiah. An Invitation to Come to the New Jerusalem 357-359

O.H. STECK (Zürich), Tritojesaja im Jesajabuch 361-406

A. ROFÉ (Jerusalem), Isaiah 59:19 and Trito-Isaiah's Vision of Redemption 407-410

W.A.M. BEUKEN (Nijmegen), Servant and Herald of Good Tidings. Isaiah 61 as an Interpretation of Isaiah 40–55 . 411-442

---

1. *Kanon und Theologie. Vorarbeiten zu einer Theologie des Alten Testaments*, Neukirchen-Vluyn, 1991, 162-171.

38 1988   viii. 16-18

R.F. COLLINS (ed.), *The Thessalonian Correspondence.*
(BETL, 87), Leuven, 1990, xv-546 p.

R.F. COLLINS (Leuven), Introduction. . . . .   XI-XV

I

THE BACKGROUND

K.P. DONFRIED (Northampton, MA), 1 Thessalonians, Acts
    and the Early Paul.   3-26
C.U. MANUS (Ife), Luke's Account of Paul in Thessalonica
    (Acts 17,1-9).   27-38
F. MORGAN-GILLMAN (San Diego), Jason of Thessalonica
    (Acts 17,5-9).   39-49
J. PLEVNIK (Toronto), Pauline Presuppositions   50-61
J. GILLMAN (San Diego), Paul's Εἴσοδος: The Proclaimed
    and the Proclaimer (1 Thes 2,8)   62-70

II

THE WRITING OF A FIRST LETTER

A. VANHOYE (Rome), La composition de 1 Thessaloniciens .   73-86
H. BINDER (Sibiu), Paulus und die Thessalonicherbriefe . .   87-93
F.W. HUGHES (Philadelphia), The Rhetoric of 1 Thessalo-
    nians   94-116
W. WUELLNER (Berkeley), The Argumentative Structure of
    1 Thessalonians as Paradoxical Encomium   117-136
I. BROER (Siegen), »Der ganze Zorn ist schon über sie
    gekommen«: Bemerkungen zur Interpolationshypothese
    und zur Interpretation von 1 Thes 2,14-16   137-159
C.M. TUCKETT (Manchester), Synoptic Tradition in 1 Thessalo-
    nians?.   160-182
J. LAMBRECHT (Leuven), Thanksgivings in 1 Thessalonians 1–3   183-205
R. KIEFFER (Lund), L'eschatologie en 1 Thessaloniciens dans
    une perspective rhétorique   206-219
J. CHAPA (Navarra), Consolatory Patterns? 1 Thes 4,13.18;
    5,11   220-228

H.J. DE JONGE (Leiden), The Original Setting of the Χριστός
ἀπέθανεν ὑπέρ Formula. 229-235
P.-E. LANGEVIN (Québec), L'intervention de Dieu selon
1 Thes 5,23-24 236-256

III
ITS THOUGHT

I.H. MARSHALL (Aberdeen), Election and Calling to Salvation in 1 and 2 Thessalonians 259-276
M.A. GETTY (Washington, DC), The Imitation of Paul in the Letters to the Thessalonians 277-283
T. HOLTZ (Halle), The Judgment on the Jews and the Salvation of All Israel. 1 Thes 2,15-16 and Rom 11,25-26. . 284-294
U. SCHNELLE (Erlangen), Die Ethik des 1. Thessalonicherbriefes. 295-305
G.P. CARRAS (Oxford), Jewish Ethics and Gentile Converts: Remarks on 1 Thes 4,3-8 306-315
N. BAUMERT (Frankfurt), Brautwerbung – das einheitliche Thema von 1 Thess 4,3-8 316-339
J. DELOBEL (Leuven), The Fate of the Dead according to 1 Thessalonians 4 and 1 Corinthians 15. 340-347
C. FOCANT (Louvain-la-Neuve), Les fils du Jour (1 Thes 5,5) 348-355
J.G. VAN DER WATT (Pretoria), The Use of ζάω in 1 Thessalonians: A Comparison with ζάω/ζωή in the Gospel of John 356-369

IV
THE WRITING OF A SECOND LETTER

M.J.J. MENKEN (Heerlen), The Structure of 2 Thessalonians 373-382
D. SCHMIDT (Fort Worth, TX), The Syntactical Style of 2 Thessalonians: How Pauline Is It? 383-393
G. HOLLAND (Allegheny), "A Letter Supposedly from Us": A Contribution to the Discussion about the Authorship of 2 Thessalonians. 394-402
F. LAUB (München), Paulinische Autorität in nachpaulinischer Zeit (2 Thes). 403-417
A. VAN AARDE (Pretoria), The Struggle against Heresy in the Thessalonian Correspondence and the Origin of the Apostolic Tradition 418-425

R.F. COLLINS (Leuven), "The Gospel of Our Lord Jesus" (2 Thes 1,8): A Symbolic Shift of Paradigm 426-440

H. KOESTER (Cambridge, MA), From Paul's Eschatology to the Apocalyptic Schemata of 2 Thessalonians 441-458

C.H. GIBLIN (New York), 2 Thessalonians 2 Re-read as Pseud-epigraphal: A Revised Reaffirmation of *The Threat to Faith* 459-469

L. HARTMAN (Uppsala), The Eschatology of 2 Thessalonians as Included in a Communication 470-485

F. DANKER (Chicago) – R. JEWETT (Evanston, IL), Jesus as the Apocalyptic Benefactor in Second Thessalonians . 486-498

C. VANDER STICHELE (Leuven), The Concept of Tradition and 1 and 2 Thessalonians 499-504

E. KRENTZ (Chicago), Traditions Held Fast: Theology and Fidelity in 2 Thessalonians 505-515

A. DENAUX (ed.), *John and the Synoptics.*
(BETL, 101), Leuven, 1992, XXII-696 p.

A. DENAUX, Introduction . . . . XIII-XXII

I

F. NEIRYNCK (Leuven), John and the Synoptics: 1975-1990[1] .   3-62
C.K. BARRETT (Durham, U.K.), The Place of John and the
Synoptics within the Early History of Christian Thought .   63-79
H. THYEN (Heidelberg), Johannes und die Synoptiker. Auf der
Suche nach einem neuen Paradigma zur Beschreibung ihrer
Beziehungen anhand von Beobachtungen an Passions- und
Ostererzählungen 81-107
R. KIEFFER (Lund), Jean et Marc: convergences dans la struc-
ture et dans les détails 109-125
H. WEDER (Zürich), Von der Wende der Welt zum Semeion
des Sohnes 127-145
D.M. SMITH (Durham, NC), The Problem of John and the
Synoptics in Light of the Relation between Apocryphal and
Canonical Gospels 147-162

A. DENAUX (Leuven), The Q-Logion Mt 11,27 / Lk 10,22 and
the Gospel of John 163-199
M.D. GOULDER (Birmingham), John 1,1–2,12 and the Synoptics. Appendix: John 2,13–4,54 201-237
M.-É. BOISMARD (Jerusalem), Jean 4,46-54 et les parallèles
synoptiques 239-259
F. VOUGA (Bethel-Bielefeld), Le quatrième évangile comme
interprète de la tradition synoptique: Jean 6 261-279
U. BUSSE (Duisburg), Johannes und Lukas: Die Lazarusperi-
kope Frucht eines Kommunikationsprozesses 281-306
A. DAUER (Bayreuth), Spuren der (synoptischen) Synedriums-
verhandlung im 4. Evangelium. Das Verhältnis zu den Syn-
optikern 307-339
M. SABBE (Leuven), The Trial of Jesus before Pilate in John
and its Relation to the Synoptic Gospels[2] 341-385
R.T. FORTNA (New York), Diachronic/Synchronic: Reading
John 21 and Luke 5 387-399

II

H. Merkel (Osnabrück), Frühchristliche Autoren über Johannes und die Synoptiker 403-408

H.J. de Jonge (Leiden), The Loss of Faith in the Historicity of the Gospels: H.S. Reimarus (ca 1750) on John and the Synoptics 409-421

J. Verheyden (Leuven), P. Gardner-Smith and «The Turn of the Tide» 423-452

T.M. Dowell (Toronto), Why John Rewrote the Synoptics? 453-457

W. Roth (Evanston, MI), Mark, John and Their Old Testament Codes 458-465

G. Geiger (Wien), Die ΕΓΩ ΕΙΜΙ-Worte bei Johannes und den Synoptikern. Eine Rückfrage nach dem historischen Jesus . . . . : 466-472

C.C. Caragounis (Lund), The Kingdom of God in John and the Synoptics: Realized or Potential Eschatology? 473-480

M. de Jonge (Leiden), The Radical Eschatology of the Fourth Gospel and the Eschatology of the Synoptics. Some Suggestions 481-487

P. Hofrichter (Salzburg), Johannesprolog und lukanische Vorgeschichte 488-497

J. Painter (Bundoora Victoria, Australia), Quest Stories in John and the Synoptics[3] 498-506

E. Bammel (Cambridge), Die Tempelreinigung bei den Synoptikern und im Johannesevangelium 507-513

M. Morgen (Strasbourg), Jean 3 et les évangiles synoptiques 514-522

J. Konings (Belo Horizonte, Brazil), The Dialogue of Jesus, Philip and Andrew in John 6,5-9 523-534

F. Segovia (Nashville, TN), The Journey(s) of Jesus to Jerusalem: Plotting and Gospel Intertextuality 535-541

B. Lindars (Manchester), Rebuking the Spirit: A New Analysis of the Lazarus Story of John 11[4] 542-547

C. Breytenbach (Berlin), MNHMONEYEIN. Das «Sich-Erinnern» in der urchristlichen Überlieferung. Die Bethanienepisode (Mk 14,3-9 / Jn 12,1-8) als Beispiel 548-557

I. Dunderberg (Helsinki), Zur Literarkritik von Joh 12,1-11 558-570

M. Menken (Heerlen, NL), The Quotations from Zech 9,9 in Mt 21,5 and in Jn 12,15 571-578

P. Létourneau (Montréal), Le quatrième évangile et les pré-
dictions de la passion dans les évangiles synoptiques 579-586

W. Schenk (Eppstein), Die Um-Codierungen der matthäischen
Unser-Vater-Redaktion in Joh 17 587-607

J. Karavidopoulos (Thessaloniki), L'heure de la crucifixion
de Jésus selon Jean et les Synoptiques. Mc 15,25 par rapport
à Jn 19,14-16 608-613

W.L. Craig (Kraainem), The Disciples' Inspection of the
Empty Tomb (Lk 24,12.24; Jn 20,2-10) 614-619

C.P. Bammel (Cambridge), The First Resurrection Appear-
ance to Peter: John 21 and the Synoptics 620-631

B. Standaert (Brugge), Jean 21 et les Synoptiques. L'enjeu
interecclésial de la dernière rédaction de l'évangile 632-643

1. *Evangelica III* (BETL, 150), 2001, 3-64.

2. *Studia Neotestamentica* (BETL, 98), 467-513.

3. Compare *The Quest for the Messiah: The History, Literature and Theology of the Johannine Community*, Edinburgh, 1991, 129-173.

4. Short version of the article *Rebuking the Spirit* (same title), published in *NTS* 38 (1992)
89-104; = *Essays on John* (SNTA, 17), Leuven, 1992, 183-198.

40 1991

A.S. VAN DER WOUDE (ed.), *The Book of Daniel in the Light of New Findings.*
(BETL, 106), Leuven, 1993, XVIII-574 p.

A.S. VAN DER WOUDE, Introduction . . . . XIII-XVIII

I
BILINGUALISM AND GREEK VERSIONS

A.S. VAN DER WOUDE (Groningen), Die Doppelsprachigkeit des Buches Daniel 3-12
P.-M. BOGAERT (Louvain-la-Neuve), Daniel 3 LXX et son supplément grec 13-37
J. LUST (Leuven), The Septuagint Version of Daniel 4–5 . . . 39-53

II
LITERARY-CRITICAL, FORM-CRITICAL AND
TRADITION-CRITICAL PROBLEMS

D. DIMANT (Haifa), The Seventy Weeks Chronology (Dan 9,24-27) in the Light of New Qumranic Texts 57-76
K. KOCH (Hamburg), Gottes Herrschaft über das Reich des Menschen. Daniel 4 im Licht neuer Funde 77-119
J.J. COLLINS (Chicago, IL), Stirring up the Great Sea: The Religio-Historical Background of Daniel 7 121-136
E. HAAG (Trier), Der Menschensohn und die Heiligen (des) Höchsten. Eine literar-, form- und traditionsgeschichtliche Studie zu Daniel 7 137-185
L. DEQUEKER (Leuven), King Darius and the Prophecy of Seventy Weeks, Daniel 9 187-210
P.W. COXON (St. Andrews, Scotland), Another Look at Nebuchadnezzar's Madness 211-222
J.W. VAN HENTEN (Leiden), Antiochus IV as a Typhonic Figure in Daniel 7 223-243
H.-F. RICHTER (Berlin), Daniel 4,7-14: Beobachtungen und Erwägungen 244-248
F.H. POLAK (Tel Aviv), The Daniel Tales in their Aramaic Literary Milieu 249-265
I. FRÖHLICH (Budapest), Daniel 2 and Deutero-Isaiah 266-270
G.G. LABONTÉ (Ottawa), Genèse 41 et Daniel 2: question d'origine 271-284
J.B. DOUKHAN (Berrien Springs, MI), Allusions à la création dans le livre de Daniel 285-292

III
LITERARY AND SOCIOLOGICAL APPROACHES

J. GOLDINGAY (Nottingham, UK), Story, Vision, Interpretation: Literary Approaches to Daniel 295-313
A. LACOCQUE (Chicago, IL), The Socio-Spiritual Formative Milieu of the Daniel Apocalypse 315-343
P. R. DAVIES (Sheffield), Reading Daniel Sociologically 345-361

IV
GENERAL HISTORICAL AND RELIGIO-HISTORICAL PROBLEMS

M. DELCOR, L'histoire selon le livre de Daniel, notamment au chapitre XI 365-386
C.C. CARAGOUNIS (Lund), History and Supra-History: Daniel and the Four Empires 387-397
M.A. KNIBB (London), "You are indeed wiser than Daniel". Reflections on the Character of the Book of Daniel . . . 399-411
D. MICHEL (Mainz), Weisheit und Apokalyptik 413-434
R.G. KRATZ (Zürich), Reich Gottes und Gesetz im Danielbuch und im werdenden Judentum 435-479
R. STAHL (Eisenach), "Eine Zeit, Zeiten und die Hälfte einer Zeit": Die Versuche der Eingrenzung der bösen Macht im Danielbuch 480-494
A. VAN DER KOOIJ (Leiden), The Concept of Covenant (Berît) in the Book of Daniel 495-501

V
OTHER STUDIES

P. DAVID (Pampanga, Philippines), Daniel 11,1: A Late Gloss? . . 505-514
B. BECKING (Utrecht), "A Divine Spirit is in You": Notes on the Translation of the Phrase rûᵃh ᵉlahîn in Daniel 5,14 and Related Texts 515-519
F. RAURELL (Barcelona), The Doxa of the Seer in Dan-LXX 12,13 520-532
J. VAN GOUDOEVER (Amsterdam), Time Indications in Daniel that Reflect the Usage of the Ancient Theoretical So-Called Zadokite Calendar 533-538
C.T. BEGG (Washington, DC), Daniel and Josephus: Tracing Connections 539-545

41 1992 viii. 18-20

C. FOCANT (ed.), *The Synoptic Gospels: Source Criticism and the New Literary Criticism.*
(BETL, 110), Leuven, 1993, XXXIX-670 p.

HOMAGE FRANS NEIRYNCK

C. FOCANT, Introduction XIII
J. DELOBEL, Professor F. Neirynck: 1960-1992 . . . . . . XV-XX
F. VAN SEGBROECK, Het Jubileumnummer BETL 100 . . . . XXI-XXV
C.M. TUCKETT, The Four Gospels 1992. Festschrift for Professor
   F. Neirynck . . . . XXVI-XXXIII
F. NEIRYNCK, Dankwoord . . . . XXXIV-XXXIX

THE SYNOPTIC GOSPELS

C. FOCANT, Introduction 3-8

MAIN PAPERS

F. NEIRYNCK (Leuven), Literary Criticism: Old and New . . . 11-38
C. FOCANT (Louvain-la-Neuve), Mc 7,24-31 par. Mt 15,21-29:
   critique des sources et/ou étude narrative 39-75
C. BREYTENBACH (Berlin), Das Markusevangelium als traditions-
   gebundene Erzählung? Anfragen an die Markusforschung
   der achtziger Jahre 77-110
V.K. ROBBINS (Atlanta, GA), Progymnastic Rhetorical Composition and Pre-Gospel Traditions: A New Approach . . . 111-147
C.M. TUCKETT (Manchester), Mark and Q 149-175
C.P. MÄRZ (Erfurt), Zur Q-Rezeption in Lk 12,35–13,35 (14,1-
   24). Die Q-Hypothese und ihre Bedeutung für die Interpreta-
   tion des lukanischen Reiseberichtes 177-208
H. MERKLEIN (Bonn), Mk 16,1-8 als Epilog des Markusevangeliums 209-238
D. MARGUERAT (Lausanne), La construction du lecteur par le
   texte (Marc et Matthieu) 239-262
J.D. KINGSBURY (Richmond, VA), The Significance of the Cross
   within the Plot of Matthew's Gospel: A Study in Narrative
   Criticism 263-279
H. FRANKEMÖLLE (Paderborn), Das Matthäusevangelium als heilige Schrift und die heilige Schrift des früheren Bundes. Von
   der Zwei-Quellen- zur Drei-Quellen-Theorie 281-310

V. Fusco (Napoli), Le discours eschatologique lucanien: "rédaction" et "composition" (Lc 21,5-36 et Mc 13,1-37) . . . 311-355
A. Denaux (Leuven), The Delineation of the Lucan Travel Narrative within the Overall Structure of the Gospel of Luke 357-392
F. Bovon (Genève), Le récit lucanien de la passion de Jésus (Lc 22–23) 393-423

OFFERED PAPERS

T.A. Friedrichsen (Sioux City, IA), Alternative Synoptic Theories on Mk 4,30-32 427-450
P. Rolland (Reims), Lecture par couches rédactionnelles de l'épisode de l'épileptique (Mc 9,14-29 et parallèles) . . . 451-458
H.B. Green (Mirfield), Matthew 11,7-15: Redaction or Self-Redaction? 459-466
E. Bammel (Cambridge), Der Anfang des Spruchbuchs . . . 467-475
W. Schenk (Dudweiler), Die Verwünschung der Küstenorte Q 10,13-15: Zur Funktion der konkreten Ortsangaben und zur Lokalisierung von Q 477-490
W.R. Telford (Newcastle), Mark and the Historical-Critical Method: The Challenge of Recent Literary Approaches to the Gospel 491-502
H. Klein (Sibiu), Zur Methode der Erforschung vormarkinischer Quellen 503-517
B. Orchard (London), The Publication of Mark's Gospel . . 518-520
B.M.F. van Iersel (Nijmegen), Concentric Structures in Mk 2,1–3,6 and 3,7-4,1: A Case Study 521-530
J. Delorme (Annecy), Signification d'un récit et comparaison synoptique (Marc 9,14-29 et parallèles) 531-547
C.B. Amphoux (Montpellier), La "finale longue de Marc": un épilogue des quatre évangiles 548-555
R. Kühschelm (Wien), Angelophanie – Christophanie in den synoptischen Grabesgeschichten Mk 16,1-8 par. (unter Berücksichtigung von Joh 20,11-18) 556-565
J.-M. van Cangh (Louvain-la-Neuve), Évolution du motif de la foi dans les miracles synoptiques, johanniques et apocryphes 566-578
D. Lührmann (Marburg), Ein neues Fragment des Petrusevangeliums 579-581
T. Baarda (Amsterdam), Clement of Alexandria and the Parable of the Fisherman: Mt 13,47-48 or Independent Tradition? . 582-598
M.H. de Lang (Leiden), Gospel Synopses from the 16th to the 18th Centuries and the Rise of Literary Criticism of the Gospels 599-607

42 1993   viii. 24-26

W.A.M. BEUKEN (ed.), *The Book of Job.*
(BETL, 114), Leuven, 1994, x-490 p.

MAIN PAPERS

D.J.A. CLINES (Sheffield), Why Is there a Book of Job and
What Does It Do To You if You Read It?   1-20
H.-P. MÜLLER (Münster), Die Hiobrahmenerzählung und ihre
altorientalischen Parallelen als Paradigmen einer weisheit-
lichen Wirklichkeitswahrnahme   21-39
W.A.M. BEUKEN (Leuven), Job's Imprecation as the Cradle of
a New Religious Discourse. The Perplexing Impact of the
Semantic Correspondences between Job 3, 4–5, 6–7 . .   41-78
J.E. HARTLEY (Azusa, CA), From Lament to Oath: A Study of
Progression in the Speeches of Job.   79-100
J. VERMEYLEN (Bruxelles), Le méchant dans les discours des
amis de Job   101-127
L.G. PERDUE (Fort Worth, TX), Metaphorical Theology in the
Book of Job: Theological Anthropology in the First Cycle
of Job's Speeches (Job 3, 6–7, 9–10)   129-156
W.L. MICHEL (Chicago, IL), Confidence and Despair: A Study
of Job 19,25-27 in the Light of Northwest Semitic Studies   157-181
J. VAN OORSCHOT (Marburg), Hiob 28: Die verborgene Weis-
heit und die Furcht Gottes als Überwindung einer gene-
ralisierten *ḥåkmå*   183-201
J. LÉVÊQUE (Paris), L'interprétation des discours de YHWH
(Job 38,1–42,6)   203-222
E.J. VAN WOLDE (Tilburg), Job 42,1-6: The Reversal of Job   223-250
N. FERNÁNDEZ MARCOS (Madrid), The Septuagint Reading of
the Book of Job   251-266
C. MANGAN (Dublin), The Interpretation of Job in the Targums   267-280
J. WEINBERG (London), Job versus Abraham: The Quest for the
Perfect God Fearer ın Rabbinic Tradition   281-296
U. BERGES (Lima), Hiob in Lateinamerika. Der leidende
Mensch und der aussätzige Gott   297-317

OFFERED PAPERS

Linguistics and prosody

L.J. DE REGT (Amsterdam), Implications of Rhetorical Questions in Strophes in Job 11 and 15 321-328

E. TALSTRA (Amsterdam), Dialogue in Job 21: «Virtual Quotations» or Text Grammatical Markers? 329-348

Redaction and tradition history

M. WITTE (Forchheim), Die dritte Rede Bildads (Hiob 25) und die Redaktionsgeschichte des Hiobbuches 349-355

H.-M. WAHL (Marburg), Das «Evangelium» Elihus (Hiob 32–37) 356-361

M. OEMING (Bonn), Hiob 31 und der Dekalog 362-368

Specific passages

W. VOGELS (Ottawa), Job's Empty Pious Slogans (Job 1,20-22; 2,8-10) 369-376

J. HOLMAN (Tilburg), Does My Redeemer Live or Is My Redeemer the Living God? Some Reflections on the Translation of Job 19,25 377-381

D. WOLFERS (Jerusalem), Job 15,4.5: An Exploration . . . 382-386

—, Job 26: An Orphan Chapter 387-391

J. DAY (Oxford), How Could Job Be an Edomite? 392-399

'Wirkungsgeschichte'

J. JOOSTEN (Bruxelles), La macrostructure du livre de Job et quelques parallèles (Jérémie 45; 1 Rois 19) 400-404

F.V. REITERER (Salzburg), Das Verhältnis Ijobs und Ben Siras 405-429

M. GOREA (Paris), Job 7,8: une contribution à la problématique des versets portant astérisque dans la Septante 430-435

C.T. BEGG (Washington, D.C.), Comparing Characters: The Book of Job and the *Testament of Job* 436-446

43 1994   viii. 8-10

R. Bieringer (ed.), *The Corinthian Correspondence*.
(BETL, 125), Leuven, 1996, xxvii-793 p.

R. Bieringer, Introduction . . . . xiii-xxvii

MAIN PAPERS

R. Bieringer (Leuven), Zwischen Kontinuität und Diskonti-
nuität. Die beiden Korintherbriefe in ihrer Beziehung
zueinander   3-38
R.F. Collins (Washington, DC), Reflections on 1 Corinthians
as a Hellenistic Letter   39-61
A. Lindemann (Bielefeld), Die paulinische Ekklesiologie
angesichts der Lebenswirklichkeit der christlichen
Gemeinde in Korinth   63-86
J.S. Vos (Amsterdam), Die Argumentation des Paulus in 1
Kor 1,10–3,4   87-119
J.-M. Sevrin (Louvain-la-Neuve), La gnose à Corinthe. Que-
tions de méthode et observations sur 1 Co 1,17–3,3   . .   121-139
F. Neirynck (Leuven), The Sayings of Jesus in 1 Corinthians   141-176
J. Delobel (Leuven), Coherence and Relevance of 1 Cor
8–10   177-190
W. Schrage (Bonn), Einige Hauptprobleme der Diskussion
des Herrenmahls im 1. Korintherbrief   191-198
C. Focant (Louvain-la-Neuve), 1 Corinthiens 13. Analyse
rhétorique et analyse de structures   199-245
C.M. Tuckett (Manchester), The Corinthians Who Say "There
is no resurrection of the dead" (1 Cor 15,12)   247-275
S. Hafemann (Wheaton, IL), Paul's Argument from the Old
Testament and Christology in 2 Cor 1–9:   277-303
D.-A. Koch (Münster), Abraham und Mose im Streit der
Meinungen. Beobachtungen und Hypothesen zur Debatte
zwischen Paulus und seinen Gegnern in 2 Kor 11,22-23
und 3,7-18   305-324

J. LAMBRECHT (Leuven), Dangerous Boasting. Paul's Self-
Commendation in 2 Cor 10–13   325-346
M.E. THRALL (Bangor), Paul's Journey to Paradise. Some
Exegetical Issues in 2 Cor 12,2-4   347-363

OFFERED PAPERS

C.J.A. HICKLING (Sheffield), Paul's Use of Exodus in the
Corinthian Correspondence   367-376
V. KOPERSKI (Miami, FL), Knowledge of Christ and Know-
ledge of God in the Corinthian Correspondence   377-396
B.J. KOET (Utrecht), As Close to the Synagogue as Can Be.
Paul in Corinth (Acts 18,1-18)   397-415
E. VERHOEF (Hollandsche Rading), The Senders of the Letters
to the Corinthians and the Use of "I" and "We" . . .   417-425
E. VERHOEF (Hollandsche Rading), Die holländische Radikale
Kritik   427-432

D.H. LIEBERT (Spokane, WA) The "Apostolic Form of Wri-
ing". Group Letters Before and After 1 Corinthians . .   433-440
T.L. BRODIE (Dublin), The Systematic Use of the Pentateuch
in 1 Corinthians   441-457
P.J. TOMSON (Bruxelles), La première épître aux Corinthiens
comme document de la tradition apostolique de halakha .   459-470
E. REINMUTH (Naumburg), LAB 40,4 und die Krise der
Weisheit im 1. Korintherbrief   471-478
G. STEYN (Johannesburg), Reflections on τὸ ὄνομα τοῦ
κυρίου in 1 Corinthians   479-490
J. VERHEYDEN (Leuven), Origen on the Origin of 1 Cor 2,9 .   491-511
B.S. ROSNER (Aberdeen) The Function of Scripture in 1 Cor
5,13b and 6,16   513-518

J. GUNDRY-VOLF (Pasadena, CA), Controlling the Bodies. A
Theological Profile of the Corinthian Sexual Ascetics
(1 Cor 7) 519-541
C.C. CARAGOUNIS (Lund), "Fornication" and "Concession"?
Interpreting 1 Cor 7, 1-7 543-560
H.-F. RICHTER (Berlin), Anstößige Freiheit in Korinth. Zur Lite
arkritik der Korintherbriefe (1 Kor 8,1-13 und 11,2-16) . 561-575
J.F.M. SMIT (Utrecht), 1 Cor 8,1-6: A Rhetorical *Partitio*. A
Contribution to the Coherence of 1 Cor 8,1–11,1 . . . 577-591
A. DENAUX (Leuven), Theology and Christology in 1 Cor
8,4-6. A Contextual-Redactional Reading 593-606
B.J. KOET (Utrecht), The Old Testament Background to 1 Cor
10,7-8 607-615
N. BAUMERT (Frankfurt), Κοινωνία τοῦ αἵματος τοῦ Χριστοῦ
(1 Kor 10,14-22) 617-622
J.-M. VAN CANGH (Louvain-la-Neuve), Peut-on reconstituer
le texte primitif de la Cène? (1 Co 11,23-26 par. Mc
14,22-26) 623-637
M.C. DE BOER (Manchester), Paul's Use of a Resurrection
Tradition in 1 Cor 15,20-28 639-651
J. HOLLEMAN (Leiden), Jesus' Resurrection as the Beginning
of the Eschatological Resurrection (1 Cor 15,20) . . . 653-660
S. SCHNEIDER (Frankfurt), 1 Kor 15,51-52. Ein neuer Lösungs-
vorschlag zu einer alten Schwierigkeit 661-669

N.M. WATSON (Flemington, Vic, Australia) "Physician, Heal
Thyself"? Paul's Character as Revealed in 2 Corinthians . 671-678
J. SCHRÖTER (Berlin), Der Apostolat des Paulus als Zugang zu
seiner Theologie. Eine Auslegung von 2 Kor 4,7-12 . . 679-692
S.E. PORTER (London), Reconciliation and 2 Cor 5,18-21 . 693-705
R.K. MOORE (Murdoch, WA, Australia), 2 Cor 5,21: The
Interpretative Key to Paul's Use of δικαιοσύνη θεοῦ? . 707-715
C. HEIL (Bamberg), Die Sprache der Absonderung in 2 Kor
6,17 und bei Paulus 717-730

44 1995

M. VERVENNE (ed.), *Studies on the Book of Exodus: Redaction - Reception - Interpretation.* (BETL, 126), Leuven, 1996, XI-660 p.

M. VERVENNE, Introduction   1-18

MAIN PAPERS

M. VERVENNE (Leuven), Current Tendencies and Developments in the Study of the Book of Exodus   21-59
E. OTTO (Mainz), Die nachpriesterschriftliche Pentateuchredaktion im Buch Exodus   61-111
F. POLAK (Tel Aviv), Theophany and Mediator: The Unfolding of a Theme in the Book of Exodus   113-147
G. FISCHER (Innsbruck), Exodus 1–15. Eine Erzählung . .   149-178
P. WEIMAR (Münster), Exodus 1,1–2,10 als Eröffnungskomposition des Exodusbuches   179-208
J. LUST (Leuven), Exodus 6,2-8 and Ezekiel   209-224
W.H. SCHMIDT (Bonn), Die Intention der beiden Plagenerzählungen (Exodus 7–10) in ihrem Kontext   225-243
W. JOHNSTONE (Aberdeen), From the Sea to the Mountain, Exodus 15,22–19,2: A Case Study in Editorial Techniques   245-263
E. ZENGER (Münster), Wie und wozu die Tora zum Sinai kam: Literarische und theologische Beobachtungen zu Exodus 19–34   265-288
J.L. SKA (Rome), Exode 19,3b-6 et l'identité de l'Israël postexilique   289-317
J. VAN SETERS (Chapel Hill, NC), Cultic Laws in the Covenant Code (Exodus 20,22–23,33) and their Relationship to Deuteronomy and the Holiness Code . . .   319-345
E. BLUM (Augsburg), Das sog. »Privilegrecht« in Exodus 34,11-26: Ein Fixpunkt der Komposition des Exodusbuches?   347-366

A. SCHENKER (Fribourg), Drei Mosaiksteinchen: »Königreich
von Priestern«, »Und ihre Kinder gehen weg«, »Wir tun
und wir hören« (Exodus 19,6; 21,22; 24,7)   367-380

C. HOUTMAN (Kampen), Eine schwangere Frau als Opfer
eines Handgemenges (Exodus 21,22-25): Ein Fall von
stellvertretender Talion im Bundesbuch?   381-397

P.-M. BOGAERT (Louvain-la-Neuve), L'importance de la Septante et du «Monacensis» de la Vetus Latina pour
l'exégèse du livre de l'Exode (chap. 35–40)   399-428

OFFERED PAPERS

Literary Criticism and Redaction History

H.-F. RICHTER (Berlin), Gab es einen »Blutbräutigam«?
Erwägungen zu Ex 4,24-26   433-441

B. LEMMELIJN (Leuven), Setting and Function of Exod 11,1-10
in the Exodus Narrative   443-460

J. WAGENAAR (Utrecht), Crossing the Sea of Reeds (Exod
13–14) and the Jordan (Josh 3–4): A Priestly Framework
for the Wilderness Wandering   461-470

A. WÉNIN (Louvain-la-Neuve), La théophanie au Sinaï:
Structures littéraires et narration en Ex 19,10–20,21 .   471-480

H. AUSLOOS (Leuven), Deuteronomi(sti)c Elements in Exod
23, 20-33? Some Methodological Remarks   481-500

S. VAN DEN EYNDE (Leuven), Keeping God's Sabbath: אות
and ברית (Exod 31,12-17)   501-511

Narrative Analysis and Linguistics

L.J. DE REGT (Amsterdam), Aspects of the Syntax and Rhetoric
of Participant Reference in Exodus   515-522

E. TALSTRA (Amsterdam), Reconstructing the *menorah* on
Disk: Some Syntactic Remarks   523-533

Intertextuality and Wirkungsgeschichte

J. Cook (Stellenbosch), Exodus 38 and Proverbs 31: A Case
of Different Order of Verses and Chapters in the Septuagint 537-549
T. Hieke (Bamberg), Der Exodus in Psalm 80: Geschichts-
topik in den Psalmen 551-558
A. van der Wal (Kampen), Themes from Exodus in Jere-
miah 30–31 559-566
J.T.A.G.M. van Ruiten (Groningen), The Relationship
between Exod 31,12-17 and Jubilees 2,1.17-33 . . . 567-575
C. Begg (Washington, DC), The Golden Calf Episode
According to Pseudo-Philo 577-594
L. Teugels (Utrecht), Did Moses See the Chariot? The
Link between Exod 19–20 and Ezek 1 in Early Jewish
Interpretation 595-602
R. Dietzfelbinger (Beuron), Ex 17,8-16 in der frühchrist-
lichen Exegese: Einige Anmerkungen 603-607

45 1996   vii. 31 - viii. 2

C.M. TUCKETT (ed.), *The Scriptures in the Gospels.*
(BETL, 131), Leuven, 1997, XXIV-721 p.

C.M. TUCKETT, Introduction . . . .   XIII-XXIV

MAIN PAPERS

C.M. TUCKETT (Oxford), Scripture and Q   3-26
F. NEIRYNCK (Leuven), Q 6,20b-21; 7,22 and Isaiah 61 . .   27-64
J. LUST (Leuven), Mic 5,1-3 in Qumran and in the New Tes-
    tament, and Messianism in the Septuagint   65-88
D. SENIOR (Chicago), The Lure of the Formula Quotations:
    Re-assessing Matthew's Use of the Old Testament with
    the Passion Narrative as Test Case   89-115
W. WEREN (Utrecht), Jesus' Entry into Jerusalem: Matthew
    21,1-17 in the Light of the Hebrew Bible and the Sep
    tuagint   117-141
C. FOCANT (Louvain-la-Neuve), La recontextualisation d'Is
    6,9-10 en Mc 4,10-12, ou un example de non-citation . 143-175
J. MARCUS (Glasgow), Scripture and Tradition in Mark 7 .   177-195
C. BREYTENBACH (Berlin), Das Markusevangelium, Psalm
    110,1 und 118,22f. Folgetext und Prätext   197-222
A.Y. COLLINS (Chicago), The Appropriation of the Psalms of
    Individual Lament by Mark 223-241
P.-M. BOGAERT (Louvain-la-Neuve), Luc et les Écritures dans
    l'Évangile de l'Enfance à la lumière des "Antiquités
    Bibliques": Histoire sainte et livres saints 243-270
A. DENAUX (Leuven), Old Testament Models for the Lukan
    Travel Narrative: A Critical Survey 271-305
M. MORGEN (Strasbourg), Lc 17,20-37 et Lc 21,8-11.20-24:
    Arrière-fond scripturaire 307-326

M. THEOBALD (Tübingen), Schriftzitate im "Lebensbrot"-
Dialog Jesu (Joh 6). Ein Paradigma für den Schriftge-
brauch des vierten Evangelisten 327-366
M.J.J. MENKEN (Utrecht), The Use of the Septuagint in Three
Quotations in John: Jn 10,34; 12,38; 19,24 367-393
U. BUSSE (Essen), Die Tempelmetaphorik als ein Beispiel von
implizitem Rekurs auf die biblische Tradition im Johannes-
evangelium 395-428

OFFERED PAPERS

M. RESE (Münster), "Intertextualität" – Ein Beispiel für Sinn
und Unsinn "neuer" Methoden 431-439
J. SCHRÖTER (Berlin), Erwägungen zum Gesetzverständnis in
Q anhand von Q 16, 16-18 441-458
N. TAYLOR (Swaziland), Interpretation of Scripture as an Indi-
cator of Socio-historical Context: The Case of Eschato-
logical Discourses of Mark and Q 459-467
T.L. BRODIE (Dublin), Intertextuality and Its Use in Tracing Q
and Proto-Luke 469-477
G. GEIGER (Wien), Falsche Zitate bei Matthäus und Lukas . 479-486
M. HASITSCHKA (Innsbruck), Die Verwendung der Schrift in
Mt 4,1-11 487-490
Lena LYBAEK (Durham), Matthew's Use of Hosea 6,6 in the
Context of the Sabbath Controversies 491-499
Susan GRAHAM (Sheffield), A Strange Salvation: Intertextual
Allusion in Mt 27,39-43 501-511
B.J. KOET (Amsterdam), Mk 12,28-34: Übereinstimmung im
Kern der Sache 513-523
J. VERHEYDEN (Leuven), Describing the Parousia: The Cosmic
Phenomena in Mk 13,24-25 525-550
G. STEYN (South Africa), Luke's Use of $MIMH\Sigma I\Sigma$? Re-
opening the Debate 551-557

F. Noël (Leuven), The Double Commandment of Love in Lk
  10,27 559-570
E. Verhoef (Hollandsche Rading), Eternal Life and Following
  the Commandments: Lev 18,5 and Lk 10,28 571-577
S. von Stemm (Berlin), Der betende Sünder vor Gott: Lk
  18,9-14. Zur Rezeption von Psalm 51(50),19 579-589
R.L. Brawley (Chicago), Scripture Resisting the Carnivales-
  que in the Lucan Passion 591-595
H.A.J. Kruger (Durban), A Sword over His Head or in His
  Hand? (Luke 22,35-38) 597-604
G.P. Carras (Berkeley), A Pentateuchal Echo in Jesus'
  Prayer on the Cross: Intertextuality between Numbers
  15,22-31 and Luke 23,34a 605-616
G. Van Belle (Leuven), L'accomplissement de la parole de
  Jésus: La parenthèse de Jn 18,9 617-627
W. Kraus (Erlangen), Die Vollendung der Schrift nach Joh
  19,28. Überlegungen zum Umgang mit der Schrift im
  Johannesevangelium 629-636
K.-W. Niebuhr (Leipzig), Die Werke des eschatologischen
  Freudenboten. 4Q521 und die Jesusüberlieferung . . . 637-646
P.J. Tomson (Brussels), The Core of Jesus' Evangel:
  εὐαγγελίσασθαι πτωχοῖς (Isa 61) 647-658

46 1997 vii. 30 - viii. 1

A. Schoors (ed.), *Qohelet in the Context of Wisdom.* (BETL, 136), Leuven, 1998, xi-529 p.

A. Schoors, Introduction 1-13

MAIN PAPERS

A. Schoors (Leuven), Words Typical of Qohelet 17-39
N. Lohfink (Frankfurt a.M.) Ist Kohelets הבל-Aussage erkenntnistheoretisch gemeint? 41-59
I.J.J. Spangenberg (Pretoria), A Century of Wrestling with Qohelet: The Research History of the Book Illustrated with a Discussion of Qoh 4,17-5,6 61-91
D. Michel (Mainz) »Unter der Sonne«: Zur Immanenz bei Qohelet 93-111
A. Lange (Tübingen), In Diskussion mit dem Tempel: Zur Auseinandersetzung zwischen Kohelet und weisheitlichen Kreisen am Jerusalemer Tempel 113-159
M. Gilbert (Namur), Qohelet et Ben Sira 161-179
L. Schwienhorst-Schönberger (Passau), Via media: Koh 7,15-18 und die griechisch-hellenistische Philosophie . 181-203
J.L. Crenshaw (Durham, NC), Qoheleth's Understanding of Intellectual Inquiry 205-224
M.V. Fox (Madison, WI), The Inner Structure of Qohelet's Thought 225-238
R.N. Whybray (Ely, Cambs), Qoheleth as a Theologian . . 239-265
J.-M. Auwers (Louvain-la-Neuve), Problèmes d'interprétation de l'épilogue de Qohèlèt 267-282
F. Vinel (Strasbourg), Le texte grec de l'Ecclésiaste et ses caractéristiques: une relecture critique de l'histoire de la royauté 283-302
P. Beentjes (Utrecht), "Who is like the Wise?": Some Notes on Qohelet 8,1-15 303-315

OFFERED PAPERS

T. HIEKE (Bamberg), Wie hast du's mit der Religion?
Sprechhandlungen und Wirkintentionen in Kohelet
4,17-5,6   319-338

A.A. FISCHER (Jena), Kohelet und die frühe Apokalyptik:
Eine Auslegung von Koh 3,16-21   339-356

L. WILSON (Melbourne), Artful Ambiguity in Ecclesiastes
1,1-11   357-365

R.W. BYARGEON (New Orleans), The Significance of Ambiguity in Ecclesiastes 2,24-26   367-372

J.Y.S. PAHK (Puchon City), The Significance of אשר in Qoh
7,26: "More bitter than death is the woman, if she is a
snare"   373-383

K.A.D. SMELIK (Brussel), A Re-Interpretation of Ecclesiastes
2,12b   385-389

A. VONACH (Innsbruck), Gottes Souveränität anerkennen:
Zum Verständnis der »Kanonformel« in Koh 3,14 . . .   391-397

H.A.J. KRUGER (Durban, South-Africa), Old Age Frailty versus Cosmic Deterioration? A Few Remarks on the Inter
pretation of Qohelet 11,7-12,8   399-411

A.J.O. VAN DER WAL (Hoofddorp), Qohelet 12,1a: A Rela-
tively Unique Statement in Israel's Wisdom Tradition .   413-418

N. KAMANO (Richmond, VA), Character and Cosmology:
Rhetoric of Qoh 1,3-3,9   419-424

E.S. CHRISTIANSON (Chester), Qoheleth and the/his Self
among the Deconstructed   425-433

H.-F. RICHTER (Berlin), Kohelet – Philosoph und Poet . . .   435-449

T.A. PERRY (Beer-Sheva/New Haven), Kohelet's Minimalist
Theology   451-456

V. D'ALARIO (Napoli), Liberté de Dieu ou destin? Un autre
dilemme dans l'interprétation du Qohélet   457-463

D. RUDMAN (London), The Anatomy of the Wise Man: Wisdom, Sorrow and Joy in the Book of Ecclesiastes . . .   465-471

A. GIANTO (Roma), Human Destiny in Emar and Qohelet . .   473-479

J. COOK (Stellenbosch), Aspects of the Relationship between
the Septuagint Versions of Kohelet and Proverbs   481-492

47 1998   vii. 29-31

J. VERHEYDEN (ed.), *The Unity of Luke-Acts*.
(BETL, 142), Leuven, 1999, xxv-828 p.

J. VERHEYDEN, Introduction . . . .   XIII-XXV

MAIN PAPERS

J. VERHEYDEN (Leuven), The Unity of Luke-Acts. What Are
   We Up To?   3-56
D. MARGUERAT (Lausanne), Luc-Actes: une unité à construire   57-81
J. DELOBEL (Leuven), The Text of Luke-Acts. A Confron-
   tation of Recent Theories   83-107
R.L. BRAWLEY (Chicago), Abrahamic Covenant Traditions
   and the Characterization of God in Luke-Acts   109-132
C.M. TUCKETT (Oxford), The Christology of Luke-Acts . . .   133-164
J.A. FITZMYER (Washington), The Role of the Spirit in Luke-
   Acts 165-183
M. RESE (Münster), The Jews in Luke-Acts. Some Second
   Thoughts 185-201
F.W. HORN (Mainz), Die Haltung des Lukas zum römischen
   Staat im Evangelium und in der Apostelgeschichte . . .   203-224
A. LINDEMANN (Bethel-Bielefeld), Einheit und Vielfalt im
   lukanischen Doppelwerk. Beobachtungen zu Reden,
   Wundererzählungen und Mahlberichten   225-253
A. DENAUX (Leuven), The Theme of Divine Visits and Human
   (In)hospitality in Luke-Acts. Its Old Testament and
   Graeco-Roman Antecedents   255-279
J. TAYLOR (Jerusalem), La fraction du pain en Luc-Actes . .   281-295
W. RADL (Augsburg), Die Beziehungen der Vorgeschichte
   zur Apostelgeschichte, dargestellt an Lk 2,22-39   297-312
O. MAINVILLE (Montréal), Le messianisme de Jésus. Le rapport
   annonce / accomplissement entre Lc 1,35 et Ac 2,33 . . .   313-327

J. KREMER (Wien), Die dreifache Wiedergabe des Damas-
kuserlebnisses Pauli in der Apostelgeschichte. Eine Hilfe
für das rechte Verständnis der lukanischen Osterevan-
gelien 329-355
F. NEIRYNCK (Leuven), Luke 4,16-30 and the Unity of Luke-
Acts 357-395

OFFERED PAPERS

D.P. MOESSNER (Dubuque, IA), The Lukan Prologues in
the Light of Ancient Narrative Hermeneutics.
Παηκολουϑηκότι and the Credentialed Author 399-417
L. ALEXANDER (Sheffield), Reading Luke-Acts from Back to
Front 419-446
S. WALTON (Nottingham), Where Does the Beginning of Acts
End? 447-467
S. VAN DEN EYNDE (Leuven), Children of the Promise. On
the Διαϑήκη-Promise to Abraham in Lk 1,72 and Acts
3,25 469-482
H. BAARLINK (Nordhorn), Die Bedeutung der Prophetenzitate
in Lk 4,18-19 und Apg 2,17-21 für das Doppelwerk des
Lukas 483-491
A. PUIG I TÀRRECH (Barcelona), Les voyages à Jérusalem
(Lc 9,51; Ac 19,21) 493-505
G. OEGEMA (Tübingen), Das Gebot der Nächstenliebe im
lukanischen Doppelwerk 507-516
V. KOPERSKI (Miami, FL), Luke 10,38-42 and Acts 6,1-7.
Women and Discipleship in the Literary Context of
Luke-Acts 517-544
M. BACHMANN (Siegen), Die Stephanusepisode (Apg
6,1–8,3). Ihre Bedeutung für die lukanische Sicht des
jerusalemischen Tempels und des Judentums 545-562
C. FOCANT (Louvain-la-Neuve), Du Fils de l'homme assis
(Lc 22,69) au Fils de l'homme debout (Ac 7,56). Enjeux
théologique et littéraire d'un changement sémantique . . 563-576

U. Schmid (Münster), Eklektische Textkonstitution als theologische Rekonstruktion. Zur Heilsbedeutung des Todes Jesu bei Lukas (Lk 22,15-20 und Apg 20,28) 577-584

P.J. Tomson (Brussel), Gamaliel's Counsel and the Apologetic Strategy of Luke-Acts 585-604

F. Wilk (Jena), Apg 10,1–11,18 im Licht der lukanischen Erzählung vom Wirken Jesu 605-617

B. Schwank (Beuron), »Das Wort des Herrn geht aus von Jerusalem« (Jes 2,3). Warum wurde das Apostelkonzil nach vorn gezogen? (Apg 15) 619-625

T.L. Brodie (Dublin), The Unity of Proto-Luke 627-638

A. del Agua (Madrid), The Lucan Narrative of the "Evangelization of the Kingdom of God". A Contribution to the Unity of Luke-Acts 639-661

G. Geiger (Wien), Der Weg als roter Faden durch Lk-Apg . 663-673

D. Bechard (New York), The Theological Significance of Judaea in Luke-Acts 675-691

G.P. Carras (Berkeley, CA), Observant Jews in the Story of Luke and Acts. Paul, Jesus and Other Jews 693-708

N.H. Taylor (Mutare), Luke-Acts and the Temple 709-721

G. Wasserberg (Kiel), Lk-Apg als Paulusapologie 723-729

J. Pichler (Graz), Das theologische Anliegen der Paulusrezeption im lukanischen Werk 731-743

B.J. Koet (Utrecht), Divine Communication in Luke-Acts . 745-757

E. Plümacher (Berlin), Cicero und Lukas. Bemerkungen zu Stil und Zweck der historischen Monographie 759-775

48 1999 vii. 28-30

A. WÉNIN (ed.), *Studies in the Book of Genesis*
(BETL, 155), Leuven, 2001, XXX-645 p.

A. Wénin, Introduction . . . . XIII-XXX

MAIN PAPERS

A. WÉNIN (Louvain-la Neuve), La question de l'humain et
l'unité du livre de la Genèse 3-34
M. VERVENNE (Leuven), Genesis 1,1–2,4. The Compositional
Texture of the Priestly Overture to the Pentateuch . . . 35-79
C. DOHMEN (Regensburg), Untergang oder Rettung der Quel-
lenscheidung? Die Sintfluterzählung als Prüfstein der
Pentateuchexegese 81-104
G.I. DAVIES (Cambridge), Genesis and the Early History of
Israel. A Survey of Research 105-134
I. FISCHER (Bonn), Das Geschlecht als exegetisches Kriterium.
Zu einer genderfairen Interpretation der Erzeltern-Erzäh-
lungen 135-152
J.L. SKA (Roma), Essai sur la nature et la signification du
cycle d'Abraham (Gn 11,27–25,11) 153-177
T.C. RÖMER (Lausanne), Recherches actuelles sur le cycle
d'Abraham 179-211
A. DE PURY (Genève), Situer le cycle de Jacob. Quelques
réflexions, vingt-cinq ans plus tard 213-241
G. FISCHER (Innsbruck), Die Josefsgeschichte als Modell für
Versöhnung 243-271
D.McL. CARR (New York), Genesis in Relation to the Moses
Story. Diachronic and Synchronic Perspectives 273-295
T.L. BRODIE (Limerick), Genesis as Dialogue: Genesis'
Twenty-six Diptychs as a Key to Narrative Unity and
Meaning 297-314
J. COOK (Stellenbosch), The Septuagint of Genesis: Text
and/or Interpretation? 315-329

OFFERED PAPERS

Diachronic Approaches

M. Bauks (Montpellier), Genesis 1 als Programmschrift der
Priesterschrift (Pg) 333-345
C. Levin (München), Gerechtigkeit Gottes in der Genesis . 347-357
R. de Hoop (Groningen), The Use of the Past to Address the
Present: the Wife-Sister-Incidents (Gen 12,10-20; 20,1-18;
26,1-16) 359-369
A. Lange (Tübingen), Becherorakel und Traumdeutung. Zu
zwei Formen der Divination in der Josephsgeschichte . 371-379
H. Ausloos (Leuven), The Deuteronomist and the Account of
Joseph's Death (Gen 50,22-26) 381-395
A. Abela (Malta), Is Genesis the Introduction of the Primary
History? 397-406
B. Lemmelijn (Leuven), Genesis' Creation Narrative: the
Literary Model for the So-Called Plague-Tradition? . . 407-419
B. Gosse (Antony), Les traditions sur Abraham et sur le
jardin d'Éden en rapport avec Is 51,2-3 et avec le livre
d'Ézéchiel 421-427

Synchronic Approaches

H.A.J. Kruger (Pinetown), Subscripts to Creation: A Few
Exegetical Comments on the Literary Device of Repeti-
tion in Gen 1–11 429-445
A. Strus (Roma), Gn 2,4b–3,24: Structure et décodage du
message 447-460
D. Rudman (Exeter), A Little Knowledge is a Dangerous
Thing: Crossing Forbidden Boundaries in Gen 3–4. . . . 461-466

S. VAN DEN EYNDE (Leuven), The Missing Link. ברית in the
    Flood Narrative: Meaning and Pecularities of a Hebrew
    Key Word   467-478
P. VAN HECKE (Leuven), Shepherds and Linguists. A Cogni-
    tive-Linguistic Approach to the Metaphor "God is Shep-
    herd" in Gen 48,15 and Context   479-493
D. ELGAVISH (Tel-Aviv), The Encounter of Abram and Mel-
    chizedek King of Salem: A Covenant Establishing Cere-
    mony   495-508
G. STEINS (Osnabrück), Die Versuchung Abrahams (Gen
    22,1-19). Ein neuer Versuch   509-519
S. GILLMAYR-BUCHER (Erfurt), Genesis 24 – ein Mosaik aus
    Texten   521-532
R. KUNTZMANN (Strasbourg), Jacob et le thème de la lutte ini-
    tiatique dans le livre de la Genèse: pertinence et intérêt
    d'une lecture symboliste   533-539
J. FLEISHMAN (Tel-Aviv), Towards Understanding the Legal
    Significance of Jacob's Statement: "I will divide them in
    Jacob, I will scatter them in Israel" (Gen 49,7b)   541-559
R. PIRSON (Tilburg), The Sun, the Moon and Eleven Stars. An
    Interpretation of Joseph's Second Dream   561-568

    Ancient Jewish Tradition

E.G. DAFNI (Göttingen), אשה כי מאיש – γυνή, ὅτι ἐκ τοῦ ἀνδρὸς
    αὐτῆς (Gen 2,23). Zur Anthropologie von Genesis 1–11 .   569-584
L. TEUGELS (Utrecht), Gap Filling and Linkage in the Midrash
    on the Rebekah Cycle   585-598
C. BEGG (Washington D.C.), Josephus' Retelling of Genesis
    34   599-605

49 2000 vii. 25-27

A. LINDEMAN (ed.), *The Sayings Source Q and the Historical Jesus.*
(BETL, 158), Leuven, 2001, XXII-776 p.

A. LINDEMAN, Introduction . . . .   XIII-XXII

MAIN PAPERS

A. LINDEMANN (Bethel), Die Logienquelle Q. Fragen an eine
gut begründete Hypothese   3-26
J. M. ROBINSON (Claremont, CA), The Critical Edition of Q
and the Study of Jesus   27-52
F. NEIRYNCK (Leuven), The Reconstruction of Q and IQP /
CritEd Parallels   53-147
J.S. KLOPPENBORG VERBIN (Toronto), Discursive Practices in
the Sayings Gospel Q and the Quest of the Historical Jesus .   149-190
D. LÜHRMANN (Marburg), Die Logienquelle und die Leben-
Jesu-Forschung   191-206
J. SCHRÖTER (Hamburg), Die Frage nach dem historischen
Jesus und der Charakter historischer Erkenntnis   207-254
P. HOFFMANN (Bamberg), Mutmaßungen über Q. Zum Problem
der literarischen Genese von Q   255-288
J. SCHLOSSER (Strasbourg), Q et la christologie implicite . .   289-316
R.A. PIPER (St. Andrews), Jesus and the Conflict of Powers in
Q: Two Miracle Stories   317-349
D. ZELLER (Mainz), Jesus, Q und die Zukunft Israels . . .   351-369
C.M. TUCKETT (Oxford), The Son of Man and Daniel 7: Q
and Jesus   371-394
D.C. ALLISON (Pittsburgh, PA), Q's New Exodus and the His-
torical Jesus   395-428
A. DENAUX (Leuven), The Parable of the Talents/Pounds (Q
19,12-27). A Reconstruction of the Q Text   429-460
J.-M. SEVRIN (Louvain-la-Neuve), Thomas, Q et le Jésus de
l'histoire   461-476

OFFERED PAPERS

L.E. VAAGE (Toronto), Jewish Scripture, Q and the Historical
Jesus: A Cynic Way with the Word?   479-495
T. HOLMÉN (Åbo), Knowing about Q and Knowing about Jesus.
Mutually Exclusive Undertakings?   497-514
A. JÄRVINEN (Helsinki), Jesus as a Community Symbol in Q .   515-521
M. TIWALD (Wien), Der Wanderradikalismus als Brücke zum
historischen Jesus   523534
M. FRENSCHKOWSKI (Mainz), Galiläa oder Jerusalem?
Die topographischen und politischen Hintergründe der
Logienquelle   535-559
M. C. MORELAND (Montgomery, AL), Q and the Economics of
Early Roman Galilee   561-575
J.-P. MICHAUD (Ottawa), Quelle(s) communauté(s) derrière la
Source Q?   577-606
C. MARUCCI (Napoli), Sprachliche Merkmale der Q-Quelle
als Hilfe für deren geschichtliche Einordnung   607-615
M. LABAHN (Wendeburg), Jesu Exorzismen (Q 11,19-20) und
die Erkenntnis der ägyptischen Magier (Ex 8,15) . .   617-633
M. HÜNEBURG (Leipzig), Jesus als Wundertäter. Zu einem
vernachlässigten Aspekt des Jesusbildes von Q . . .   635-648
C. HEIL (Bamberg), Beobachtungen zur theologischen
Dimension der Gleichnisrede Jesu in Q   649-659
W.J.C. WEREN (Tilburg), From Q to Matthew 22,1-14. New
Light on the Transmission and Meaning of the Parable of
the Guests   661-679
A. PUIG I TÀRRECH (Barcelona), Une parabole à l'image
antithétique 6,46-49   681-693
J. VERHEYDEN (Leuven), The Conclusion of Q: Eschatology in
Q 22,28-30   695-718
E. BROADHEAD (Berea, KY), The Extent of the Sayings
Tradition (Q)   719-728
T. BRODIE (Limerick), An Alternative Q/Logia Hypothesis:
Deuteronomy-based, Qumranlike, Verifiable   729-743

50 2001

J.-M. AUWERS (Louvain-la-Neuve) & H.J. de Jonge (Leiden),
The Biblical Canons.

F. NEIRYNCK, Colloquium Biblicum Lovaniense: 1-50.

MAIN PAPERS

T. SÖDING (Wuppertal), Der Kanon des Alten und Neuen Testaments.

A. VAN DER KOOIJ (Leiden), Canonization of Ancient Hebrew Books and Hasmonaean Politics.

E. ULRICH (Notre Dame, IN), Qumran and the Canon of the Old Testament.

J. LUST (Leuven), The Septuagint and the Canon of the Old Testament.

E. ZENGER (Münster), Der Psalter im Horizont von Tora und Prophetie. Kanonisch-intertextuelle Perspektiven.

G. DORIVAL (Aix-Marseille), L'apport des Pères de l'Église à la question de la clôture du Canon de l'Ancien Testament.

J. ZUMSTEIN (Zürich), La naissance de la notion d'Écriture dans la littérature johannique.

J. SCHRÖTER (Berlin), Betrachtungen zur Aufnahme der Apostelgeschichte in den Kreis kanonischer Schriften.

A. LINDEMANN (Bethel), Zeugnisse für die Sammlung der Paulusbriefe im 1. und 2. Jahrhundert.

G. STANTON (Cambridge), Aspects of the Use of Gospel Traditions in the Second Century.

J. VERHEYDEN (Leuven), Canon and Scripture in the Canon Muratori: A Matter of Dispute.

SEMINARS

J. BARTON (Oxford), Canonical Criticism Ancient and Modern.

G. STEINS (Bamberg), Der Bibelkanon – Sammlung, Text, oder was sonst? Methodologische Probleme kanonischer Schriftauslegung.

C.M. TUCKETT (Oxford), The Gospels in the History of the New Testament Canon.

K.-W. NIEBUHR (Jena), Exegese im kanonischen Zusammenhang: Überlegungen zur theologischen Relevanz der Gestalt des neutestamentlichen Kanons.

P.-M. BOGAERT (Maredsous – Louvain-la-Neuve), Aux origines de la fixation du canon: scriptoria, listes et titres.

M. DE JONGE (Leiden), Het gezag van het "Oude Testament" in de vroege kerk: het getuigenis van de "pseudepigrapha van het Oude Testament".

LIST OF CONTRIBUTORS

* President of the session

ABELA, A.   1999
ACKROYD, P.R.   1974
ALAND, K.   1971
ALAND, B.   1986
ALETTI, J.N.   1984
ALEXANDER, L.   1998
ALFRINK, B.   1958, 1974
ALLISON, D.C.   2000
AMPHOUX, C.B.   1992
AMSLER, S.   1978, 1983, 1987
ANBAR, M.   1983
ANDRIESSEN, P.   1962
ANGÉNIEUX, J.   1967
ARENS, A.   1960
ARNALDICH, L.   1958
ASVELD, P.   1966
AUSLOOS, H.   1995, 1999
AUVRAY, P.   1958
AUWERS J.-M.   1997, 2001*

BAARDA, T.   1981, 1986, 1992
BAARLINK, H.   1998
BACHMANN, M.   1998
BAILLET, M.   1960, 1976
BALTZER, D.   1985
BAMMEL, C.P.   1990
BAMMEL, E.   1977, 1990, 1992
BANKS, M.   1999
BARR, J.   1972
BARRETT, C.K.   1974, 1977, 1984, 1990
BARTHÉLEMY, D.   1957, 1963
BARTON, J.   2001
BARTSCH, H.W.   1971
BARUCQ, A.   1974
BAUER, J.-B.   1958
BAUKS, M.   1999
BAUMERT, N.   1984, 1988, 1994
BEASLEY-MURRAY, G.R.   1979
BEATRICE, P.F.   1986
BEAUCHAMP, P.   1978, 1987
BECHARD, D.   1998
BECKER, J.   1985

BECKING, B.   1991
BEENTJES, P.C.   1987, 1997
BEGG, C.T.   1983, 1985, 1987,
   1991, 1993, 1995, 1999
BENOIT, P.   1958, 1973
BERÉNYI, G.   1984
BERGES, U.   1993
BERNINI, G.   1958
BEST, E.   1971
BETZ, H.D.   1984
BETZ, O.   1957
BEUKEN, W.A.M.   1980, 1987,
   1993*
BEUTLER, J.   1986
BIERINGER, R.   1994*
BINDER, H.   1988
BLACK, M.   1969
BLÄSER, P.   1958
BLUM, E.   1995
BOADT, L.   1985
BÖCHER, O.   1979
BOGAERT, P.-M.   1969, 1976, 1979,
   1980*, 1983, 1985, 1987, 1991,
   1995, 1996, 2001
BOISMARD, M.-É.   1958, 1971, 1975,
   1986, 1990
BONNARD, P.   1965, 1974, 1975
BONNARD, P.-É.   1978
BORGEN, P.   1975
BOUWMAN, G.   1968 (²1989)
BOVATI, P.   1987
BOVON, F.   1977, 1992
BRAULIK, G.   1983
BRAUN, F.-M.   1954, 1956*, 1958,
   1961
BRAWLEY, R.L.   1996, 1998
BREKELMANS, C.   1958, 1963,
   1972*, 1978, 1980, 1983, 1987
BREYTENBACH, C.   1990, 1992, 1996
BROADHEAD, E.   2000
BRODIE, T.L.   1994, 1996, 1998,
   1999, 2000

BROER, I.   1988
BROWN, R.E.   1966*, 1975
BROWNLEE, H.W.   1976
BRUNET, A.-M.   1958
BRUNET, G.   1980
BUCHANAN, G.W.   1981
BUIS, P.   1982
BURCHARD, C.   1969
BUSA, R.   1958
BUSSE, U.   1990, 1996
BYARGEON, R.W.   1997

CAHILL, J.   1966
CAMBIER, J.   1955, 1959
CAPELLE, B.   1958
CAQUOT, A.   1976
CARAGOUNIS, C.C.   1990, 1991,
   1994
CARLSTON, C.E.   1981
CARMIGNAC, J.   1976
CARR, D.M.   1999
CARRAS, G.P.   1988, 1996, 1998
CARREZ, M.   1988
CAUBET ITURBE, J.   1958
CAZELLES, H.   1958, 1963, 1967*,
   1974, 1978, 1980, 1983
CERFAUX, L.   1949*, 1952, 1955,
   1956, 1957, 1958, 1962, 1968
CHAPA, J.   1988
CHARBEL, A.   1958
CHARUE, A.-M.   1952, 1958, 1967
CHRISTENSEN, D.L.   1983
CHRISTIANSON, E.S.   1997
CLEMENTS, R.E.   1985, 1987
CLINES, D.J.A.   1993
COLLINS, A.Y.   1979, 1996
COLLINS, J.J.   1991
COLLINS, R.F.   1979, 1988*, 1994
COOK, J.   1995, 1997, 1999
COPPENS, J.   1949, 1950*, 1952,
   1956, 1957, 1958*, 1959, 1960,
   1961, 1962, 1963, 1966, 1967,
   1968, 1971, 1974*, 1975, 1976,
   1977, 1978, 1979
COTHENET, É.   1970
COXON, P.W.   1991
CRAIG, W.L.   1990
CRENSHAW, J.L.   1978, 1997

DAFNI, E.G.   1999

DAHOOD, M.   1958, 1967, 1972
D'ALARIO, V.   1997
DANKER, F.   1988
DAUER, A.   1990
DAUTZENBERG, G.   1984
DAVID, P.   1991
DAVIES, G.I.   1987, 1999
DAVIES, P.R.   1991
DAY, J.   1993
DE AUSEJO, S.   1958
DE BOER, M.C.   1994
DE BOER, P.A.H.   1972
DE FRAINE, J.   1958, 1960
DEHANDSCHUTTER, B.   1968, 1969,
   1971, 1977, 1979, 1981, 1986
DE HOOP, R.   1999
DEISSLER, A.   1958
DE JONG, C.   1980
DE JONGE, H.J.   1988, 1990, 2001*
DE JONGE, M.   1973, 1975*, 1979,
   1990, 2001
DEL AGUA, A.   1998
DE LANG, M.H.   1992
DE LANGHE, R.   1952, 1954, 1958,
   1959*, 1963
DE LA POTTERIE, I.   1956, 1958,
   1965*, 1973, 1975
DELCOR, M.   1960, 1969, 1974,
   1976*, 1991
DE LEEUW, V.   1952
DELOBEL, J.   1968, 1975, 1979,
   1981*, 1984, 1986, 1988, 1992,
   1994, 1998
DELORME, J.   1965, 1992
DE MENASCE, J.   1958
DENAUX, A.   1968, 1981, 1990*,
   1992, 1994, 1996, 1998, 2000
DENIS, A.-M.   1965
DE PURY, A.   1999
DEQUEKER, L.   1972, 1991
DE REGT, L.J.   1993, 1995
DESCAMPS, A.-L.   1952, 1955, 1958,
   1959*, 1960, 1967, 1968, 1970,
   1971, 1973
DE SOLAGES, B.   1955
DEVISCH, M.   1970, 1971
DIDIER, M.   1965, 1970*
DIETZFELBINGER, R.   1995
DIJKSTRA, M.   1985
DIMANT, D.   1991

DOEVE, J.W.   1955, 1969
DOHMEN, C.   1985, 1999
DONFRIED, K.P.   1974, 1975, 1988
DORIVAL, G.   2001
DOSSIN, G.   1954
DOUKHAN, J.B.   1991
DOWELL, T.M.   1990
DRIOTON, É.   1958
DRIVER, G.R.   1954
DUBARLE, A.-M.   1958, 1963, 1967
DUMAIS, M.   1977
DUNCKER, G.   1958
DUNDERBERG, I.   1990
DUNGAN, D.L.   1971
DUPLACY, J.   1958, 1968
DUPONT, J.   1958, 1960, 1968, 1970, 1973*, 1977, 1981

EDWARDS, R.A.   1981
ELGAVISH, D.   1999
ELLIS, E.E.   1968, 1973

FABRY, H.-J.   1976, 1983
FEUILLET, A.   1958, 1961
FERNÁNDEZ MARCOS, N.   1993
FIORENZA, E. SCHÜSSLER   1979
FISCHER, A.A.   1997
FISCHER, G.   1995, 1999
FISCHER, I.   1999
FITZMYER, J.A.   1973, 1998
FLEISHMAN, J.   1999
FOCANT, C.   1988, 1992*, 1994, 1996, 1998
FOHRER, G.   1978
FORTNA, R.T.   1990
FOX, M.V.   1997
FRANKEMÖLLE, H.   1992
FRANQUESA, P.   1958
FRENSCHKOWSKI, M.   2000
FRIEDRICHSEN, T.A.   1968 ([2]1989) 1992
FRÖHLICH, I.   1991
FUHS, H.F.   1985
FULLER, R.H.   1977
FUSCO, V.   1981, 1992

GARCÍA DE LA FUENTE, O.   1958
GARCÍA LÓPEZ, F.   1983
GATZWEILER, K.   1970
GEIGER, G.   1990, 1996, 1998

GELIN, A.   1958
GEORGE, A.   1958, 1965, 1973
GESCHÉ, A.   1974
GETTY, M.A.   1988
GEYSER, A.S.   1979
GIANTO, A.   1997
GIBLET, J.   1952, 1956, 1962*, 1974, 1975
GIBLIN, C.H.   1988
GIL ULECIA, A.   1958
GILBERT, M.   1974, 1978*, 1980, 1997
GILLMAN, J.   1988
GILLMAYER-BUCHER, S.   1999
GILS, F.   1958
GITAY, Y.   1987
GOLDINGAY, J.   1991
GONZALEZ RUIZ, J.-M.   1958
GOOSSENS, G.   1958
GOREA, M.   1993
GOSSE, B.   1999
GOULDER, M.D.   1990
GRÄSSER, E.   1977
GRAHAM, S.   1996
GREEN, H.B.   1992
GREENBERG, M.   1985
GRELOT, P.   1961, 1962, 1966
GRIBOMONT, J.   1949
GROSS, H.   1958, 1963
GROSSOUW, W.   1952, 1956
GUILLAUME, A.   1954
GUNDRY-VOLF, J.   1994

HAAG, E.   1991
HAAG, H.   1958
HAELEWYCK, J.-C.   1987
HAFEMANN, S.   1994
HAHN, F.   1977
HALBE, J.   1983
HAMP, V.   1958
HANHART, K.   1975
HARTLEY, J.Z.   1993
HARTMAN, L.   1970, 1979, 1988
HASITSCHKA, M.   1996
HAURET, C.   1958, 1963*
HAVET, J.   1959
HEIL, C.   1994, 2000
HELDERMAN, J.   1986
HENDRIKS, W.   1971
HENGEL, M.   1976

HENNINGER, J. 1958
HERMISSON, H.-J. 1987
HERRMANN, S. 1980
HEUSCHEN, J. 1955*
HICKLING, C.J.A. 1975, 1977, 1981, 1994
HIEKE, T. 1995, 1997
HØGENHAVEN, J. 1987
HOFBAUER, J. 1958
HOFFMANN, P. 2000
HOFRICHTER, P. 1990
HOLLADAY, W.L. 1980, 1983
HOLLAND, G. 1988
HOLLEMAN, J. 1994
HOLMAN, J. 1993
HOLMÉN, T. 2000
HOLTZ, T. 1979, 1988
HOPPE, L.J. 1983
HORN, F.W. 1998
HOSSFELD, F.L. 1985
HOUSSIAU, A. 1958, 1974
HOUTMAN, C. 1995
HUBMANN, F.D. 1980
HÜNEBURG, M. 2000

ILG, N. 1976

JACOB, E. 1967
JACOBSON, A.D. 1981
JÄRVINEN, A. 2000
JANSSEN, J.M.A. 1954
JANSSENS, Y. 1958, 1975, 1979
JAUBERT, A. 1957, 1976
JENKINS, A.K. 1987
JERVELL, J. 1977
JOHNSTONE, W. 1995
JOMIER, J. 1958
JONGELING, B. 1976
JÓNSSON, J. 1974
JOOSTEN, J. 1993
JUDGE, P.J. 1968 (^{2}1989)
JOYCE, P. 1985
JUNKER, H. 1958

KÄSEMANN, E. 1973
KAHMANN, J. 1970, 1986
KAISER, O. 1987
KAMANO, N. 1997
KARAVIDOPOULOS, J. 1990
KAUFMANN, S.A. 1983

KERRIGAN, A. 1958
KERTELGE, K. 1984
KIEFFER, R. 1988, 1990
KILPATRICK, G.D. 1977
KINGSBURY, J.D. 1992
KIRCHSCHLÄGER, W. 1977, 1984
KISSANE, E.J. 1954, 1958
KLEIN, H. 1992
KLOPPENBORG, J.S. 2000
KNIBB, M.A. 1991
KOCH, D.-A. 1994
KOCH, K. 1991
KOCH, R. 1958
KOESTER, H. 1988
KOET, B.J. 1994, 1996, 1998
KONINGS, J. 1971, 1990
KOPERSKI, V. 1994, 1998
KORTEWEG, T. 1979
KRATZ, R.G. 1991
KRAUS, W. 1996
KREMER, J. 1977*, 1998
KRENTZ, E. 1988
KRUGER, H.A.J. 1996, 1997, 1999
KÜHSCHELM, R. 1992
KÜMMEL, W.G. 1968
KUNTZMANN, R. 1999
KUTSCH, E. 1972
LABAHN, M. 2000
LABERGE, L. 1983
LABONTÉ, G.G. 1991
LABUSCHAGNE, C.J. 1983
LACH, S. 1958
LACOCQUE, A. 1991
LAMBERT, G. 1957
LAMBRECHT, J. 1965, 1970, 1971, 1977, 1979*, 1981, 1984, 1988, 1994
LANG, B. 1978, 1985
LANGE, A. 1997, 1999
LANGEVIN, P.-E. 1988
LAPERROUSAZ, F.M. 1976
LARGEMENT, R. 1958
LAUB, F. 1988
LAURENTIN, A. 1956
LE DÉAUT, R. 1967
LEFORT, T. 1958
LÉGASSE, S. 1970, 1974, 1981
LEGRAND, L. 1974
LELOIR, L. 1961
LEMAIRE, A. 1985

LEMAITRE, H. 1958
LEMMELIJN, B. 1995, 1999
LÉON-DUFOUR, X. 1955, 1965, 1973
LÉTOURNEAU, P. 1990
LÉVEQUE, J. 1972, 1978, 1993
LEVIE, J. 1951*, 1955, 1958
LEVIN, C. 1999
LICHTENBERGER, R. 1976
LIEBERT, D.H. 1994
LINDARS, B. 1975, 1990
LINDEMANN, A. 1986, 1994, 1998, 2000*, 2001
LINNEMANN, E. 1973
LIPINSKI, E. 1960
LOCHER, C. 1983
LÖVESTAM, E. 1979
LOHFINK, N. 1974, 1978, 1980, 1983*, 1997
LÜHRMANN, D. 1973, 1992, 2000
LUST, J. 1967, 1974, 1979, 1980, 1983, 1985*, 1987, 1991, 1995, 1996, 2001
LUTTIKHUIZEN, G.P. 1986
LUYTEN, J. 1978, 1983
LYBAEK, L. 1996
LYONNET, S. 1958, 1959
LYS, D. 1978

MAARSINGH, B. 1985
MÄRZ, C.P. 1992
MAGNE, J. 1981
MAINVILLE, O. 1998
MALEVEZ, L. 1966
MANGAN, C. 1993
MANUS, C.U. 1988
MARBÖCK, J. 1978
MARCUS, J. 1996
MARGUERAT, D. 1992, 1998
MARLÉ, R. 1962
MARSHALL, I.H. 1988
MARTIN, M. 1960
MARTIN, V. 1956
MARTIN-ACHARD, R. 1972
MARTINI, C.M. 1970, 1977
MARTYN, J.L. 1975
MARUCCI, C. 2000
MASSAUX, É. 1958, 1961*
MATERA, F.J. 1968 (²1989)
MAYEDA, G. 1979

MAYES, A.D.H. 1983
McCARTHY, D.J. 1972
McKANE, W. 1978
McLOUGHLIN, S. 1965
MEJÍA, J. 1958
MEN, A. 1984
MÉNARD, J.-É. 1958
MENKEN, M.J.J. 1988, 1990, 1996
MENOUD, P.-H. 1956
MERKEL, H. 1990
MERKLEIN, H. 1992
MICHAUD, J.-P. 2000
MICHEL, D. 1991, 1997
MICHEL, W.L. 1993
MILIK, J.T. 1976
MINETTE DE TILLESSE, G. 1963
MOESSNER, D.P. 1998
MOLLAT, D. 1958
MONLOUBOU, L. 1985
MOORE, R.K. 1994
MORELAND, M.C. 2000
MORGAN-GILLMAN, F. 1988
MORGEN, M. 1990, 1996
MOURLON BEERNAERT, P. 1971
MUDDIMAN, J.B. 1973
MÜLLER, H.-P. 1993
MÜLLER, P.G. 1977
MULDER, M.J. 1985
MUÑOZ IGLESIAS, S. 1958
MURPHY, R.E. 1958
MUSSIES, G. 1979

NEIRYNCK, F. 1965, 1968*, 1970, 1971, 1973, 1975, 1977, 1979, 1981, 1984, 1986, 1990, 1992, 1994, 1996, 1998, 2000, 2001
NELLESSEN, E. 1977
NIEBUHR, K.-W. 1996, 2001
NOËL, F. 1996
NOBILE, M. 1985, 1987
NÖTSCHER, F. 1957
NOORDA, S.J. 1977, 1981

OEGEMA, G. 1998
OEMING, M. 1993
O'NEIL, J.C. 1984
ORCHARD, B. 1992
OTTO, E. 1995

PABST, H. 1976

PAHK, J.Y.S.   1997
PAINTER, J.   1975, 1990
PATHRAPANKAL, J.   1977
PAUL, M.J.   1983
PEINADOR, M.   1958
PENNA, R.   1984
PERDUE, L.G.   1993
PERLITT, L.   1983
PERRIN, N.   1971
PERRY, T.A.   1997
PESCH, R.   1968, 1971, 1979
PETITJEAN, A.   1967
PHILONENKO, M.   1969
PICHLER, J.   1998
PIPER, R.A.   1981, 2000
PIRENNE, J.   1958
PIRSON, P.   1999
PLEVNIK, J.   1988
PLÜMACHER, E.   1977, 1998
POLAK, F.H.   1991, 1995
POLLARD, T.E.   1975
PONS, J.   1985
PONTHOT, J.   1984
PORTER, S.E.   1994
PRATO, G.L.   1978
PREUSS, H.D.   1972
PRIGENT, P.   1979
PUIG Ì TÀRRECH, A.   1998, 2000

QUECKE, H.   1961
QUISPEL, G.   1956

RADERMAKERS, J.   1971
RADL, W.   1984, 1998
RÄISÄNEN, H.   1981
RAMLOT, M.-L.   1966
RASCO, E.   1965
RAURELL, F.   1978, 1985, 1991
REESE, J.M.   1978
REINMUTH, E.   1994
REITERER, F.V.   1993
RENARD, H.   1958
RENAUD, B.   1980, 1985
RENDTORFF, R.   1985, 1987
RENGSTORF, K.H.   1969
RESE, M.   1973, 1977, 1979, 1984, 1996, 1998
RICHTER, H.-F.   1991, 1994, 1995, 1997
RIESENFELD, H.   1959, 1961

RIGAUX, B.   1952*, 1958, 1959, 1961, 1974.
ROBBINS, V.K.   1992
ROBERTS, J.H.   1984
ROBINSON, J.M.   1971, 1981, 2000
RÖMER, T.   1999
ROETZEL, C.J.   1984
ROFÉ, A.   1983, 1987
ROLLAND, P.   1992
ROOD, L.A.   1959
ROSE, A.   1960
ROSNER, B.S.   1994
ROTH, W.   1990
ROWLEY, H.H.   1954, 1967
RUCKSTUHL, E.   1975
RUDMAN, D.   1997, 1999
RUYSSCHAERT, J.   1958
RYCKMANS, G.   1954*, 1967

SABBE, M.   1961, 1965, 1971*, 1975, 1977, 1981, 1990
SABUGAL, S.   1976
SAMAIN, É.   1968
SAMAIN, P.   1949
SAWYER, J.F.A.   1972, 1987
SAYDON, P.-P.   1958
SCHARBERT, J.   1967, 1980
SCHEIRE, U.   1966
SCHELKLE, K.H.   1958
SCHENK, W.   1990, 1992
SCHENKER, A.   1995
SCHILDENBERGER, J.   1958
SCHLIER, H.   1959
SCHLOSSER, J.   2000
SCHMID, U.   1998
SCHMIDT, D.   1988
SCHMIDT, W.H.   1995
SCHMITT, J.   1957, 1976, 1977
SCHNACKENBURG, R.   1958, 1975
SCHNEIDER, G.   1977
SCHNEIDER, S.   1994
SCHNEIDERS, S.M.   1975
SCHNELLE, U.   1988
SCHOORS, A.   1963, 1967, 1997*
SCHRAGE, W.   1984, 1994
SCHRECK, C.J.   1968 (²1989)
SCHRÖTER, J.   1994, 1996, 2000, 2001
SCHÜRMANN, H.   1981
SCHWANK, B.   1975, 1998

SCHWEIZER, E. 1974
SCHWIENHORST-SCHÖNBERGER, L. 1997
SEGOVIA, F. 1990
SENIOR, D. 1970, 1996
SERVOTTE, H. 1974
SEVRIN, J.-M. 1981, 1986*, 1994, 2000
SEYNAEVE, J. 1974
SIMIAN-YOFRE, M. 1985
SKA, J.L. 1995, 1999
SKEHAN, P.W. 1976
SMELIK, K.A.D. 1997
SMIT, J.F.M. 1994
SMIT SIBINGA, J. 1970
SMITH, D.M. 1990
SNOY, T. 1971
SÖDING, T. 2001
SOGGIN, J.A. 1980
SPANGENBERG, I.J.J. 1997
SPICQ, C. 1958
SPOTTORNO, V. 1985
SPYKERBOER, H.C. 1987
STAHL, R. 1991
STANDAERT, B. 1984, 1990
STANTON, G. 2001
STARCKY, J. 1976
STECK, O.H. 1987
STEGEMANN, H. 1976
STEINS, G. 1999, 2001
STEMM, S. VON 1996
STEYN, G. 1994, 1996
STRECKER, G. 1970
STRUS, A. 1999
SUENENS, L. 1967
SZYSZMAN, E. 1976

TALMON, S. 1976
TALSTRA, E. 1987, 1993, 1995
TAYLOR, J. 1998
TAYLOR, N. 1996
TAYLOR, N.H. 1998
TELFORD, W.R. 1992
TESTUZ, M. 1959
TEUGELS, L. 1995, 1999
THEOBALD, M. 1996
THILS, G. 1966*, 1967
THOMAS D. WINTON 1967
THRALL, M.E. 1994
THYEN, H. 1975, 1990

TIWALD, M. 2000
TOMSON, P.J. 1994, 1996, 1998
TOV, E. 1980
TROMP, N.J. 1978, 1985, 1987
TROOSTER, S. 1966
TUCKETT, C.M. 1981, 1984, 1986, 1988, 1992, 1994, 1996*, 1998, 2000, 2001

ULRICH, E. 2001

VAAGE, L.E. 2000
VAN AARDE, A. 1988
VAN BELLE, G. 1996
van BOHEMEN, N. 1955
van CANG, J.-M. 1971, 1981, 1992, 1994
VAN DEN BERGHE, P. 1960
VAN DEN BUSSCHE, H. 1956, 1959, 1962
VAN DEN EYNDE, S. 1995, 1998, 1999
van DER KOOIJ, A. 1987, 1991, 2001
van DER PLOEG, J. 1952, 1957*, 1958, 1967, 1976, 1978
VANDER STICHELE, C. 1988
VAN DER VEKEN, J. 1974
van DER WAL, A. 1995, 1997
VAN DER WATT, J.G. 1988
van DER WOUDE, A.S. 1957, 1976, 1991*
VAN DE WALLE, B. 1958
van DIJK, A.M. 1954
van GOUDOEVER, J. 1983, 1985, 1987, 1991
van GROL, H.W.M. 1980
VAN HECKE, P. 1999
van HENTEN, J.W. 1991
VANHOYE, A. 1974, 1984*, 1988
van IERSEL, B.M.F. 1961, 1965, 1992
VAN IMSCHOOT, P. 1953*
VANNI, U. 1979
VANONI, G. 1983
van OORSCHOT, J. 1993
VAN PETEGHEM, L. 1967
VAN RIET, G. 1966
VAN ROEY, J.-E. 1958
van RUITEN, J. 1987, 1995

BIBLIOTHECA EPHEMERIDUM THEOLOGICARUM LOVANIENSIUM

● Colloquium Biblicum Lovaniense
○ Other Biblical Studies

SERIES I

* = Out of print

*1. *Miscellanea dogmatica in honorem Eximii Domini J. Bittremieux*, 1947.
*2-3. *Miscellanea moralia in honorem Eximii Domini A. Janssen*, 1948.
*4. G. PHILIPS, *La grâce des justes de l'Ancien Testament*, 1948.
*5. G. PHILIPS, *De ratione instituendi tractatum de gratia nostrae sanctificationis*, 1953.
○6-7. *Recueil Lucien Cerfaux. Études d'exégèse et d'histoire religieuse*, 1954. 504 et 577 p. Cf. *infra*, n°⁵ 18 et 71 (t. III). Par tome,   25 €
8. G. THILS, *Histoire doctrinale du mouvement œcuménique*, 1955. Nouvelle édition, 1963. 338 p.   25 €
*9. *Études sur l'Immaculée Conception*, 1955.
*10. J.A. O'DONOHOE, *Tridentine Seminary Legislation*, 1957.
*11. G. THILS, *Orientations de la théologie*, 1958.
●*12-13. J. COPPENS, A. DESCAMPS, É. MASSAUX (ed.), *Sacra Pagina. Miscellanea Biblica Congressus Internationalis Catholici de Re Biblica*, 1959.
*14. *Adrien VI, le premier Pape de la contre-réforme*, 1959.
*15. F. CLAEYS BOUUAERT, *Les déclarations et serments imposés par la loi civile aux membres du clergé belge sous le Directoire (1795-1801)*, 1960.
*16. G. THILS, *La «Théologie œcuménique». Notion-Formes-Démarches*, 1960.
17. G. THILS, *Primauté pontificale et prérogatives épiscopales. «Potestas ordinaria» au Concile du Vatican*, 1961. 103 p.   2 €
*18. *Recueil Lucien Cerfaux*, t. III, 1962. Cf. *infra*, n° 71.
*19. *Foi et réflexion philosophique. Mélanges F. Grégoire*, 1961.
*20. *Mélanges G. Ryckmans*, 1963.
21. G. THILS, *L'infaillibilité du peuple chrétien «in credendo»*, 1963. 67 p.   2 €
*22. J. FÉRIN & L. JANSSENS, *Progestogènes et morale conjugale*, 1963.
*23. *Collectanea Moralia in honorem Eximii Domini A. Janssen*, 1964.
● 24. H. CAZELLES (ed.), *De Mari à Qumrân. L'Ancien Testament. Son milieu. Ses écrits. Ses relectures juives* (Hommage J. Coppens, I), 1969. 158*-370 p.   23 €
●*25. I. DE LA POTTERIE (ed.), *De Jésus aux évangiles. Tradition et rédaction dans les évangiles synoptiques* (Hommage J. Coppens, II), 1967.
● 26. G. THILS & R.E. BROWN (ed.), *Exégèse et théologie* (Hommage J. Coppens, III), 1968. 328 p.   18 €
27. J. COPPENS (ed.), *Ecclesia a Spiritu sancto edocta. Hommage à Mgr G. Philips*, 1970. 640 p.   25 €
28. J. COPPENS (ed.), *Sacerdoce et célibat. Études historiques et théologiques*, 1971. 740 p.   18 €

● 29. M. DIDIER (ed.), *L'évangile selon Matthieu. Rédaction et théologie,* 1972.
   432 p.   25 €
*30. J. KEMPENEERS, *Le Cardinal van Roey en son temps,* 1971.

SERIES II

○ 31. F. NEIRYNCK, *Duality in Mark. Contributions to the Study of the Markan
   Redaction,* 1972. Revised edition with Supplementary Notes, 1988. 252 p.
                                                                             30 €
● 32. F. NEIRYNCK (ed.), *L'évangile de Luc. Problèmes littéraires et théologiques,*
   1973. *L'évangile de Luc – The Gospel of Luke.* Revised and enlarged
   edition, 1989. x-590 p.   55 €
● 33. C. BREKELMANS (ed.), *Questions disputées d'Ancien Testament. Méthode
   et théologie,* 1974. *Continuing Questions in Old Testament Method and
   Theology.* Revised and enlarged edition by M. VERVENNE, 1989. 245 p.
                                                                             30 €
● 34. M. SABBE (ed.), *L'évangile selon Marc. Tradition et rédaction,* 1974.
   Nouvelle édition augmentée, 1988. 601 p.   60 €
  35. B. WILLAERT (ed.), *Philosophie de la religion – Godsdienstfilosofie.
   Miscellanea Albert Dondeyne,* 1974. Nouvelle édition, 1987. 458 p.
                                                                             40 €
  36. G. PHILIPS, *L'union personnelle avec le Dieu vivant. Essai sur l'origine et
   le sens de la grâce créée,* 1974. Édition révisée, 1989. 299 p.   25 €
○ 37. F. NEIRYNCK, in collaboration with T. HANSEN and F. VAN SEGBROECK,
   *The Minor Agreements of Matthew and Luke against Mark with a Cumu-
   lative List,* 1974. 330 p.   23 €
○ 38. J. COPPENS, *Le messianisme et sa relève prophétique. Les anticipations
   vétérotestamentaires. Leur accomplissement en Jésus,* 1974. Édition
   révisée, 1989. XIII-265 p.   25 €
○ 39. D. SENIOR, *The Passion Narrative according to Matthew. A Redactional
   Study,* 1975. New impression, 1982. 440 p.   25 €
● 40. J. DUPONT (ed.), *Jésus aux origines de la christologie,* 1975. Nouvelle
   édition augmentée, 1989. 458 p.   38 €
● 41. J. COPPENS (ed.), *La notion biblique de Dieu,* 1976. Réimpression, 1985.
   519 p.   40 €
  42. J. LINDEMANS & H. DEMEESTER (ed.), *Liber Amicorum Monseigneur W.
   Onclin,* 1976. XXII-396 p.   25 €
  43. R.E. HOECKMAN (ed.), *Pluralisme et œcuménisme en recherches théologiques. Mélanges offerts au R.P. Dockx, O.P.,* 1976. 316 p.   25 €
● 44. M. DE JONGE (ed.), *L'évangile de Jean. Sources, rédaction, théologie,*
   1977. Réimpression, 1987. 416 p.   38 €
  45. E.J.M. VAN EIJL (ed.), *Facultas S. Theologiae Lovaniensis 1432-1797.
   Bijdragen tot haar geschiedenis. Contributions to its History. Contributions à son histoire,* 1977. 570 p.   43 €
● 46. M. DELCOR (ed.), *Qumrân. Sa piété, sa théologie et son milieu,* 1978.
   432 p.   43 €
  47. M. CAUDRON (ed.), *Faith and Society. Foi et société. Geloof en maat-
   schappij. Acta Congressus Internationalis Theologici Lovaniensis 1976,*
   1978. 304 p.   29 €

● 48. J. KREMER (ed.), *Les Actes des Apôtres. Traditions, rédaction, théologie,*
       1979. 590 p.   43 €
○ 49. F. NEIRYNCK, avec la collaboration de J. DELOBEL, T. SNOY, G. VAN BELLE,
       F. VAN SEGBROECK, *Jean et les Synoptiques. Examen critique de l'exégèse
       de M.-É. Boismard,* 1979. XII-428 p.   25 €
○ 50. J. COPPENS, *La relève apocalyptique du messianisme royal. I. La royauté
       – Le règne – Le royaume de Dieu. Cadre de la relève apocalyptique,*
       1979. 325 p.   25 €
● 51. M. GILBERT (ed.), *La Sagesse de l'Ancien Testament,* 1979. Nouvelle édi-
       tion mise à jour, 1990. 455 p.   38 €
  52. B. DEHANDSCHUTTER, *Martyrium Polycarpi. Een literair-kritische studie,*
       1979. 296 p.   25 €
● 53. J. LAMBRECHT (ed.), *L'Apocalypse johannique et l'Apocalyptique dans le
       Nouveau Testament,* 1980. 458 p.   35 €
● 54. P.-M. BOGAERT (ed.), *Le livre de Jérémie. Le prophète et son milieu. Les
       oracles et leur transmission,* 1981. *Nouvelle édition mise à jour,* 1997.
       448 p.   45 €
○ 55. J. COPPENS, *La relève apocalyptique du messianisme royal. III. Le Fils
       de l'homme néotestamentaire.* Édition posthume par F. NEIRYNCK, 1981.
       XIV-192 p.   20 €
  56. J. VAN BAVEL & M. SCHRAMA (ed.), *Jansénius et le Jansénisme dans les
       Pays-Bas. Mélanges Lucien Ceyssens,* 1982. 247 p.   25 €
  57. J.H. WALGRAVE, *Selected Writings – Thematische geschriften. Thomas
       Aquinas, J.H. Newman, Theologia Fundamentalis.* Edited by G. DE
       SCHRIJVER & J.J. KELLY, 1982. XLIII-425 p.   25 €
  58. F. NEIRYNCK & F. VAN SEGBROECK, avec la collaboration de E. MANNING,
       *Ephemerides Theologicae Lovanienses 1924-1981. Tables générales.
       (Bibliotheca Ephemeridum Theologicarum Lovaniensium 1947-1981),*
       1982. 400 p.   40 €.
● 59. J. DELOBEL (ed.), *Logia. Les paroles de Jésus – The Sayings of Jesus.
       Mémorial Joseph Coppens,* 1982. 647 p.   50 €
○ 60. F. NEIRYNCK, *Evangelica. Gospel Studies – Études d'évangile. Collected
       Essays.* Edited by F. VAN SEGBROECK, 1982. XIX-1036 p.   50 €
○ 61. J. COPPENS, *La relève apocalyptique du messianisme royal. II. Le Fils
       d'homme vétéro- et intertestamentaire.* Édition posthume par J. LUST,
       1983. XVII-272 p.   25 €
  62. J.J. KELLY, *Baron Friedrich von Hügel's Philosophy of Religion,* 1983.
       232 p.   38 €
  63. G. DE SCHRIJVER, *Le merveilleux accord de l'homme et de Dieu. Étude de
       l'analogie de l'être chez Hans Urs von Balthasar,* 1983. 344 p.   38 €
  64. J. GROOTAERS & J.A. SELLING, *The 1980 Synod of Bishops: «On the Role
       of the Family». An Exposition of the Event and an Analysis of its Texts.*
       Preface by Prof. emeritus L. JANSSENS, 1983. 375 p.   38 €.
○ 65. F. NEIRYNCK & F. VAN SEGBROECK, *New Testament Vocabulary. A Com-
       panion Volume to the Concordance,* 1984. XVI-494 p.   50 €
○ 66. R.F. COLLINS, *Studies on the First Letter to the Thessalonians,* 1984. XI-
       415 p.   38 €
  67. A. PLUMMER, *Conversations with Dr. Döllinger 1870-1890.* Edited with
       Introduction and Notes by R. BOUDENS, with the collaboration of L. KENIS,
       1985. LIV-360 p.   45 €

● 68. N. LOHFINK (ed.), *Das Deuteronomium. Entstehung, Gestalt und Botschaft /Deuteronomy: Origin, Form and Message*, 1985. XI-382 p.   50 €

69. P.F. FRANSEN, *Hermeneutics of the Councils and Other Studies.* Collected by H.E. MERTENS & F. DE GRAEVE, 1985. 543 p.   45 €

○ 70. J. DUPONT, *Études sur les Évangiles synoptiques.* Présentées par F. NEIRYNCK, 1985. 2 tomes, XXI-IX-1210 p.   70 €

○ 71. *Recueil Lucien Cerfaux*, t. III, 1962. Nouvelle édition revue et complétée, 1985. LXXX-458 p.   40 €

72. J. GROOTAERS, *Primauté et collégialité. Le dossier de Gérard Philips sur la Nota Explicativa Praevia (Lumen gentium, Chap. III).* Présenté avec introduction historique, annotations et annexes. Préface de G. THILS, 1986. 222 p.   25 €

● 73. A. VANHOYE (ed.), *L'apôtre Paul. Personnalité, style et conception du ministère*, 1986. XIII-470 p.   65 €

● 74. J. LUST (ed.), *Ezekiel and His Book. Textual and Literary Criticism and their Interrelation*, 1986. X-387 p.   68 €

○ 75. É. MASSAUX, *Influence de l'Évangile de saint Matthieu sur la littérature chrétienne avant saint Irénée.* Réimpression anastatique présentée par F. NEIRYNCK. *Supplément: Bibliographie 1950-1985*, par B. DEHANDSCHUTTER, 1986. XXVII-850 p.   63 €

76. L. CEYSSENS & J.A.G. TANS, *Autour de l'Unigenitus. Recherches sur la genèse de la Constitution*, 1987. XXVI-845 p.   63 €

○ 77. A. DESCAMPS, *Jésus et l'Église. Études d'exégèse et de théologie.* Préface de Mgr A. HOUSSIAU, 1987. XLV-641 p.   63 €

○ 78. J. DUPLACY, *Études de critique textuelle du Nouveau Testament.* Présentées par J. DELOBEL, 1987. XXVII-431 p.   45 €

79. E.J.M. VAN EIJL (ed.), *L'image de C. Jansénius jusqu'à la fin du XVIIIᵉ siècle*, 1987. 258 p.   32 €

80. E. BRITO, *La Création selon Schelling. Universum*, 1987. XXXV-646 p.   75 €

● 81. J. VERMEYLEN (ed.), *The Book of Isaiah – Le livre d'Isaïe. Les oracles et leurs relectures. Unité et complexité de l'ouvrage*, 1989. X-472 p.   68 €

○ 82. G. VAN BELLE, *Johannine Bibliography 1966-1985. A Cumulative Bibliography on the Fourth Gospel*, 1988. XVII-563 p.   68 €

83. J.A. SELLING (ed.), *Personalist Morals. Essays in Honor of Professor Louis Janssens*, 1988. VIII-344 p.   30 €

○ 84. M.-É. BOISMARD, *Moïse ou Jésus. Essai de christologie johannique*, 1988. XVI-241 p.   25 €

○ 84ᴬ. M.-É. BOISMARD, *Moses or Jesus: An Essay in Johannine Christology.* Translated by B.T. VIVIANO, 1993, XVI-144 p.   25 €

85. J.A. DICK, *The Malines Conversations Revisited*, 1989. 278 p.   38 €

● 86. J.-M. SEVRIN (ed.), *The New Testament in Early Christianity – La réception des écrits néotestamentaires dans le christianisme primitif*, 1989. XVI-406 p.   63 €

● 87. R.F. COLLINS (ed.), *The Thessalonian Correspondence*, 1990. XV-546 p.   75 €

○ 88. F. VAN SEGBROECK, *The Gospel of Luke. A Cumulative Bibliography 1973-1988*, 1989. 241 p.   30 €

89. G. THILS, *Primauté et infaillibilité du Pontife Romain à Vatican I et autres études d'ecclésiologie*, 1989. XI-422 p. 47 €
90. A. VERGOTE, *Explorations de l'espace théologique. Études de théologie et de philosophie de la religion*, 1990. XVI-709 p. 50 €
○*91. J.C. DE MOOR, *The Rise of Yahwism: The Roots of Israelite Monotheism*, 1990. *Revised and Enlarged Edition*, 1997. XV-445 p. 35 €
92. B. BRUNING, M. LAMBERIGTS & J. VAN HOUTEM (eds.), *Collectanea Augustiniana. Mélanges T.J. van Bavel*, 1990. 2 tomes, XXXVIII-VIII-1074 p. 75 €
93. A. DE HALLEUX, *Patrologie et œcuménisme. Recueil d'études*, 1990. XVI-887 p. 75 €
○ 94. C. BREKELMANS & J. LUST (eds.), *Pentateuchal and Deuteronomistic Studies: Papers Read at the XIIIth IOSOT Congress Leuven 1989*, 1990. 307 p. 38 €
○ 95. D.L. DUNGAN (ed.), *The Interrelations of the Gospels. A Symposium Led by M.-É. Boismard – W.R. Farmer – F. Neirynck, Jerusalem 1984*, 1990. XXXI-672 p. 75 €
○ 96. G.D. KILPATRICK, *The Principles and Practice of New Testament Textual Criticism. Collected Essays*. Edited by J.K. ELLIOTT, 1990. XXXVIII-489 p. 75 €
97. G. ALBERIGO (ed.), *Christian Unity. The Council of Ferrara-Florence: 1438/39 – 1989*, 1991. X-681 p. 75 €
○ 98. M. SABBE, *Studia Neotestamentica. Collected Essays*, 1991. XVI-573 p. 50 €
○ 99. F. NEIRYNCK, *Evangelica II: 1982-1991. Collected Essays*. Edited by F. VAN SEGBROECK, 1991. XIX-874 p. 70 €
○100. F. VAN SEGBROECK, C.M. TUCKETT, G. VAN BELLE & J. VERHEYDEN (eds.), *The Four Gospels 1992. Festschrift Frans Neirynck*, 1992. 3 volumes, XVII-X-X-2668 p. 125 €

SERIES III

●101. A. DENAUX (ed.), *John and the Synoptics*, 1992. XXII-696 p. 75 €
○102. F. NEIRYNCK, J. VERHEYDEN, F. VAN SEGBROECK, G. VAN OYEN & R. CORSTJENS, *The Gospel of Mark. A Cumulative Bibliography: 1950-1990*, 1992. XII-717 p. 68 €
103. M. SIMON, *Un catéchisme universel pour l'Église catholique. Du Concile de Trente à nos jours*, 1992. XIV-461 p. 55 €
104. L. CEYSSENS, *Le sort de la bulle Unigenitus. Recueil d'études offert à Lucien Ceyssens à l'occasion de son 90e anniversaire*. Présenté par M. LAMBERIGTS, 1992. XXVI-641 p. 50 €
105. R.J. DALY (ed.), *Origeniana Quinta. Papers of the 5th International Origen Congress, Boston College, 14-18 August 1989*, 1992. XVII-635 p. 68 €
●106. A.S. VAN DER WOUDE (ed.), *The Book of Daniel in the Light of New Findings*, 1993. XVIII-574 p. 75 €
107. J. FAMERÉE, *L'ecclésiologie d'Yves Congar avant Vatican II: Histoire et Église. Analyse et reprise critique*, 1992. 497 p. 65 €
○108. C. BEGG, *Josephus' Account of the Early Divided Monarchy (AJ 8, 212-420). Rewriting the Bible*, 1993. IX-377 p. 60 €

109. J. Bulckens & H. Lombaerts (eds.), *L'enseignement de la religion catholique à l'école secondaire. Enjeux pour la nouvelle Europe*, 1993. XII-264 p.   32 €

●110. C. Focant (ed.), *The Synoptic Gospels. Source Criticism and the New Literary Criticism*, 1993. XXXIX-670 p.   75 €

111. M. Lamberigts (ed.), avec la collaboration de L. Kenis, *L'augustinisme à l'ancienne Faculté de théologie de Louvain*, 1994. VII-455 p.   60 €

○112. R. Bieringer & J. Lambrecht, *Studies on 2 Corinthians*, 1994. XX-632 p.   75 €

113. E. Brito, *La pneumatologie de Schleiermacher*, 1994. XII-649 p.   75 €

●114. W.A.M. Beuken (ed.), *The Book of Job,* 1994. X-462 p.   60 €

○115. J. Lambrecht, *Pauline Studies: Collected Essays,* 1994. XIV-465 p.   63 €

○116. G. Van Belle, *The Signs Source in the Fourth Gospel: Historical Survey and Critical Evaluation of the Semeia Hypothesis,* 1994. XIV-503 p.   63 €

117. M. Lamberigts & P. Van Deun (eds.), *Martyrium in Multidisciplinary Perspective. Memorial L. Reekmans*, 1995. X-435 p.   75 €

○118. G. Dorival & A. Le Boulluec (eds.), *Origeniana Sexta. Origène et la Bible/Origen and the Bible. Actes du Colloquium Origenianum Sextum, Chantilly, 30 août – 3 septembre 1993*, 1995. XII-865 p.   98 €

119. É. Gaziaux, *Morale de la foi et morale autonome. Confrontation entre P. Delhaye et J. Fuchs*, 1995. XXII-545 p.   68 €

120. T.A. Salzman, *Deontology and Teleology: An Investigation of the Normative Debate in Roman Catholic Moral Theology*, 1995. XVII-555 p.   68 €

121. G.R. Evans & M. Gourgues (eds.), *Communion et Réunion. Mélanges Jean-Marie Roger Tillard*, 1995. XI-431 p.   60 €

○122. H.T. Fleddermann, *Mark and Q: A Study of the Overlap Texts*. With an *Assessment* by F. Neirynck, 1995. XI-307 p.   45 €

123. R. Boudens, *Two Cardinals: John Henry Newman, Désiré-Joseph Mercier*. Edited by L. Gevers with the collaboration of B. Doyle, 1995. 362 p.   45 €

124. A. Thomasset, *Paul Ricœur. Une poétique de la morale. Aux fondements d'une éthique herméneutique et narrative dans une perspective chrétienne*, 1996. XVI-706 p.   75 €

●125. R. Bieringer (ed.), *The Corinthian Correspondence*, 1996. XXVII-793 p.   60 €

●126. M. Vervenne (ed.), *Studies in the Book of Exodus: Redaction – Reception – Interpretation*, 1996. XI-660 p.   60 €

127. A. Vanneste, *Nature et grâce dans la théologie occidentale. Dialogue avec H. de Lubac*, 1996. 312 p.   45 €

○128. A. Curtis & T. Römer (eds.), *The Book of Jeremiah and its Reception – Le livre de Jérémie et sa réception*, 1997. 331 p.   60 €

129. E. Lanne, *Tradition et Communion des Églises. Recueil d'études*, 1997. XXV-703 p.   75 €

130. A. Denaux & J.A. Dick (eds.), *From Malines to ARCIC. The Malines Conversations Commemorated*, 1997. IX-317 p.   45 €

●131. C.M. Tuckett (ed.), *The Scriptures in the Gospels*, 1997. XXIV-721 p.   60 €

○132. J. van Ruiten & M. Vervenne (eds.), *Studies in the Book of Isaiah. Festschrift Willem A.M. Beuken,* 1997. XX-540 p.   75 €

○133. M. Vervenne & J. Lust (eds.), *Deuteronomy and Deuteronomic Literature. Festschrift C.H.W. Brekelmans,* 1997. XI-637 p.   75 €

134. G. Van Belle (ed.), *Index Generalis ETL / BETL 1982-1997,* 1999. IX-337 p.   40 €

135. G. De Schrijver, *Liberation Theologies on Shifting Grounds. A Clash of Socio-Economic and Cultural Paradigms,* 1998. XI-453 p.   53 €

●136. A. Schoors (ed.), *Qohelet in the Context of Wisdom,* 1998. XI-528 p.   60 €

137. W.A. Bienert & U. Kühneweg (eds.), *Origeniana Septima. Origenes in den Auseinandersetzungen des 4. Jahrhunderts,* 1999. XXV-848 p.   95 €

138. É. Gaziaux, *L'autonomie en morale: au croisement de la philosophie et de la théologie,* 1998. XVI-760 p.   75 €

139. J. Grootaers, *Actes et acteurs à Vatican II,* 1998. XXIV-602 p.   75 €

○140. F. Neirynck, J. Verheyden & R. Corstjens, *The Gospel of Matthew and the Sayings Source Q: A Cumulative Bibliography 1950-1995,* 1998. 2 vols., VII-1000-420* p.   95 €

141. E. Brito, *Heidegger et l'hymne du sacré,* 1999. XV-800 p.   90 €

●142. J. Verheyden (ed.), *The Unity of Luke-Acts,* 1999. XXV-828 p.   60 €

○143. N. Calduch-Benages & J. Vermeylen (eds.), *Treasures of Wisdom. Studies in Ben Sira and the Book of Wisdom. Festschrift M. Gilbert,* 1999. XXVII-463 p.   75 €

○144. J.-M. Auwers & A. Wénin (eds.), *Lectures et relectures de la Bible. Festschrift P.-M. Bogaert,* 1999. XLII-482 p.   75 €

○145. C. Begg, *Josephus' Story of the Later Monarchy (AJ 9,1–10,185),* 2000. X-650 p.   75 €

○146. J.M. Asgeirsson, K. De Troyer & M.W. Meyer (eds.), *From Quest to Q. Festschrift James M. Robinson,* 2000. XLIV-346 p.   60 €

○147. T. Römer (ed.), *The Future of the Deuteronomistic History,* 2000. XII-265 p.   75 €

148. F.D. Vansina, *Paul Ricœur: Bibliographie primaire et secondaire - Primary and Secondary Bibliography 1935-2000,* 2000. XXVI-544 p.   75 €

○149. G.J. Brooke & J.D. Kaestli (eds.), *Narrativity in Biblical and Related Texts,* 2000. XXI-307 p.   75 €

○150. F. Neirynck, *Evangelica III: 1992-2000. Collected Essays,* 2001. XVII-666 p.   60 €

○151. B. Doyle, *The Apocalypse of Isaiah Metaphorically Speaking. A Study of the Use, Function and Significance of Metaphors in Isaiah 24-27,* 2000. XII-453 p.   75 €

152. T. Merrigan & J. Haers (eds.), *The Myriad Christ. Plurality and the Quest for Unity in Contemporary Christology,* 2000. XIV-593 p.   75 €

153. M. Simon, *Le catéchisme de Jean-Paul II. Genèse et évaluation de son commentaire du Symbole des apôtres,* 2000. XVI-688 p.   75 €

○154. J. Vermeylen, *La loi du plus fort. Histoire de la rédaction des récits davidiques de 1 Samuel 8 à 1 Rois 2,* 2000. XIII-746 p.   81 €

●155. A. Wénin (ed.), *Studies in the Book of Genesis. Literature, Redaction and History,* 2001. XXX-645 p.   60 €

156. F. Ledegang, *Mysterium Ecclesiae. Images of the Church and its Members in Origen.* 2000. XVIII-722 p.   85 €

157. J.S. BOSWELL, F.P. McHUGH & J. VERSTRAETEN (eds.), *Catholic Social Thought: Twilight of Renaissance?* 2000. XXII-307 p.   60 €

●158. A. LINDEMANN (ed.), *The Sayings Source Q and the Historical Jesus.* 2001. XXII-776 P.   60 €

PRINTED ON PERMANENT PAPER • IMPRIME SUR PAPIER PERMANENT • GEDRUKT OP DUURZAAM PAPIER - ISO 9706

ORIENTALISTE, KLEIN DALENSTRAAT 42, B-3020 HERENT